Devotions with Jesus

Daily Insight from a Pastor's Heart

Devotions with Jesus

Daily Insight from a Pastor's Heart

Mike Mirakian

Copyright © 2021 Mike Mirakian

All rights reserved

No part of this book may be reproduced, or stored in a retrieval system, or transmitted in any form or by any means, electronic, mechanical, photocopying, recording, or otherwise, without express written permission of the publisher.

ISBN: 9798748841368

Printed in the United States of America

Scriptures taken from the Holy Bible, New International Version®, NIV®. Copyright © 1973, 1978, 1984, 2011 by Biblica, Inc.™ Used by permission of Zondervan. All rights reserved worldwide. www.zondervan.com The "NIV" and "New International Version" are trademarks registered in the United States Patent and Trademark Office by Biblica, Inc.™

DEDICATION

To my family and church
who care for me
and allow me to teach God's word.

CONTENTS

Preface	i
The Birth of Jesus	1
The Sermon on the Mount	33
The Parables of Jesus	77
Jesus' Death and Resurrection	175

PREFACE

When the world shut down in March 2020 to slow the spread of COVID-19, our church made the difficult but wise decision to stop gathering in person. Like many churches, we had to scramble to figure out online options to help our congregation worship and hear God's word from home. Thankfully, we were able to resume in-person ministries by July 2020, with limited capacities and other safeguards in place. Over the next year, as the pandemic stretched on and vaccines became available, we saw our church slowly return to usual patterns of fellowship, worship, Bible study and all the many ways we share life together. I praise God that our church has largely weathered this difficult storm with patience, love for one another, generosity and wisdom. God has blessed us, and in turn, we have been able to bless those around us.

Early on, when we were not gathering together, one of our church leaders suggested that I write devotions to send out to the congregation. It was a great idea, and I began sending three devotions each week. Initially, I planned to stop writing these once we were able to gather again for Bible studies and worship, but the response from our church was so positive that I have continued to write.

This book includes the devotions I wrote from the Gospels, covering Jesus' birth, the Sermon on the Mount, Jesus' parables, and the story of our Savior's death and resurrection. I believe in the power of God's word to change hearts, so it's His word, not mine, that matters. I hope what I have written will help you follow God's word, drawing you closer to Jesus.

If you are new to faith or if you don't yet know what it means to follow Jesus, I trust these devotions will help you hear God's truth in new and meaningful ways. Maybe as you read, you will feel drawn to Jesus and want to accept the new and eternal life only He can give you. If so, choosing to follow Jesus is as simple as saying Thank you, Sorry and Please.

Tell God, "Thank You for loving me and for sending Jesus to be my Savior. I'm sorry for all the ways I have hurt You and hurt those around me. Please forgive me and fill me with Your Spirit so I can follow Jesus all my life. Please give me the assurance of eternal life in Jesus' name."

THE BIRTH OF JESUS

Jesus came to seek and save the lost. To accomplish his great mission of grace, Jesus had to enter our world and our humanity, joining us in the flesh of human existence so He could then redeem us through his death and resurrection. We begin our devotional journey at the beginning of Jesus' journey among us: his birth as a humble child. It's the Christmas story that we know and love. Matthew and Luke tell us how Jesus' birth came about, and we begin with John's poetic, theological insights into who Jesus is and why He came. May this familiar story speak anew to your heart.

John 1:1-5

In the beginning was the Word, and the Word was with God, and the Word was God. He was with God in the beginning. Through him all things were made; without him nothing was made that has been made. In him was life, and that life was the light of all mankind. The light shines in the darkness, and the darkness has not overcome it.

I wonder how long it took John, under the Spirit's inspiration, to settle on these particular word-images to describe the indescribable. John knew Jesus personally. He heard him teach, witnessed many of Jesus' miracles, and was there when Jesus calmed the storm and later when He walked on water. John saw Jesus die on the cross, and then talked with him after the resurrection. So, when John sat down to write his account of Jesus' life, I wonder what went through his mind as he chose these words. John decided to call Jesus "the Word" and "the light," images rich in Biblical meaning and poetic weight. Of the four Gospel writers, maybe of all New Testament authors, John was the best wordsmith, able to make mysterious truths understandable. Nowhere is that more evident or more important than in the opening lines to his Gospel.

John didn't tell the Christmas story. He didn't mention Mary and Joseph or the shepherds or the manger where Jesus slept his first night. Instead, John wanted his readers to know that Jesus is God and has been with God from "the beginning." That is, Jesus has always existed as God and with God, there before this world was created, there to participate fully and powerfully in the Creation. John wanted us to know that Jesus existed before all things and that his birth into this world was not his beginning. Jesus came into the world that He helped create, bringing life-giving light to all humanity. Those are deep and heavy ideas that John's words have carried into the hearts of believers for 2,000 years.

As we consider Jesus' birth, we need to remember, with John, that Jesus came to bring light into darkness. We also need to take hold as firmly and as faithfully as we can of John's declaration that the darkness has not overcome the light. We cling to that truth, even in the face of so much lingering trouble and despair in our broken, hurting world. Jesus brings us the undimming light of God's goodness that shines just as gloriously today as it did when the world was made through him. Don't allow the darkness to overshadow you. Turn your heart, instead, to the Light and to the good news of our Savior's birth.

Jesus, I believe You are God and that You have existed from before all time. I believe You came into this world to bring light to my heart and to everyone who believes. Help me reflect Your light to others so they can find their way to You. I pray in Your name. Amen.

John 1:6-13

There was a man sent from God whose name was John. He came as a witness to testify concerning that light, so that through him all might believe. He himself was not the light; he came only as a witness to the light.

The true light that gives light to everyone was coming into the world. He was in the world, and though the world was made through him, the world did not recognize him. He came to that which was his own, but his own did not receive him. Yet to all who did receive him, to those who believed in his name, he gave the right to become children of God—children born not of natural descent, nor of human decision or a husband's will, but born of God.

We start to see them every year around Thanksgiving. Through front windows and along rooflines, around trees and in once dark corners of our homes, we see the little twinkling lights of Christmas. Even people who don't understand what those lights represent enjoy their soft glow and warm sparkle. Christmas lights, from old wax candles to modern LED bulbs, help tell the story of Jesus' birth, just as John the Baptist came as a witness to the light of Christ. Don't dismiss the power of this symbol. Jesus is the true light that gives light to everyone, and all the shining decorations of the Christmas season point people toward that True Light, even those who don't yet believe in the Savior or his birth.

These verses don't let us forget about those who are still lost in sin. Our Christmas traditions may revolve around our love for Jesus and our joy at his birth, but Jesus came, like light shining into darkness, to seek and save the lost. He entered the world He created, the world He owns, for the sake of sinners, for people who have rejected God's goodness and have never even thought to ask for a Savior. Jesus came for people like us who, without the faithful witness of a parent or friend or pastor or neighbor, would still be lost in sin. There was a time when we didn't recognize him as our Savior. There was a time when we didn't understand or appreciate the True Light. Now, we rejoice because we know the good news, and so, like John the Baptist, we testify to those in need concerning the light.

There's another great and wonderful mystery about the light of Christ. Like the Christmas lights that shine from houses and stores during the holiday season, the light Jesus brought into this dark world "gives light to everyone." Some don't yet believe. Some struggle with sin and doubt. Some have heard and rejected the truth. Some believe and rejoice. But the light shines all around to everyone, just as God sends rain on the just and the unjust, and causes the sun to shine down on all people, giving us warmth and light. In theological terminology, this goodness shared by all humanity is known as common grace. We see it reflected in the Christmas lights that give everyone a little bit of brightness and joy. How much more, then, do we see God's goodness in Jesus who came to offer everyone the hope of rebirth!

Father in Heaven, thank You for sending Jesus into the world and for bringing Your light into my heart. Help me to share this good news with others as I rejoice in Jesus' birth. Amen.

John 1:14-18

The Word became flesh and made his dwelling among us. We have seen his glory, the glory of the one and only Son, who came from the Father, full of grace and truth.

(John testified concerning him. He cried out, saying, "This is the one I spoke about when I said, 'He who comes after me has surpassed me because he was before me.'") Out of his fullness we have all received grace in place of grace already given. For the law was given through Moses; grace and truth came through Jesus Christ. No one has ever seen God, but the one and only Son, who is himself God and is in closest relationship with the Father, has made him known.

With whom have you made your dwelling? We don't use that word often today, and you would probably get a strange look if you were to ask a new neighbor, "Where did you dwell before you moved here?" In one sense, your dwelling is simply the place where you currently reside. It's your house and more broadly your neighborhood and community. The word John chose actually has roots in the act of pitching a tent, and more specifically in Biblical language, to setting up a tabernacle. This points back to the Tabernacle where God's presence dwelt among the Israelites during their wilderness wanderings and for the many generations before Solomon built the Temple in Jerusalem. The Tabernacle was God's dwelling place, not just a tent set up for a night in the desert, but a place that symbolized God's glory and power among his people. Where they went, God went. Where they set up their tents, God made his dwelling in the Tabernacle.

So, Jesus took on our flesh, took on the real, physical reality of our human bodies, and He made his dwelling among us. Jesus' physical body became the tabernacle in which the glory of God resided for those few years of Jesus' earthly life. God pitched his tent among us in the person of Jesus. There's much more we could unwind theologically about how Jesus' incarnation fulfilled the prophetic promise of the Tabernacle and Temple, but we also need to remember that Jesus' dwelling among us was not just a temporary arrangement. Jesus didn't just pitch his tent on earth for a few years and then move away. He came to stay, to dwell here among us for as long as this world lasts and then into eternity. Jesus no longer walks around in a physical body, limited to one place at a time. Now, He dwells in our hearts, through the presence of his Holy Spirit. Now, God tabernacles with you, with me and with all faithful followers of Jesus.

What a blessing it is to love the God who dwells among his people! He's not a far off, distant, uninvolved deity floating up in the clouds. No, our God walks with us. He speaks to us. He carries us when we are weak. He touches us with healing and comfort. He dwells in our hearts. Jesus became flesh to reveal God's grace and truth, and his Spirit dwells among us still.

Father in Heaven, You revealed Your love for me and all people when You sent Jesus into the world. Thank You for choosing to dwell in my life through Your Holy Spirit. Teach me to feel Your presence, hear Your voice and follow Your leading each day. I pray in Jesus' name. Amen.

Luke 1:26-33

In the sixth month of Elizabeth's pregnancy, God sent the angel Gabriel to Nazareth, a town in Galilee, to a virgin pledged to be married to a man named Joseph, a descendant of David. The virgin's name was Mary. The angel went to her and said, "Greetings, you who are highly favored! The Lord is with you."

Mary was greatly troubled at his words and wondered what kind of greeting this might be. But the angel said to her, "Do not be afraid, Mary; you have found favor with God. You will conceive and give birth to a son, and you are to call him Jesus. He will be great and will be called the Son of the Most High. The Lord God will give him the throne of his father David, and he will reign over Jacob's descendants forever; his kingdom will never end."

Advent is a season of waiting. We wait for Christmas to arrive. We wait to open presents under the tree. We wait for visits from family members traveling from far away. We wait for traditions to be renewed and enjoyed by younger generations. We also remember what it was like for the world to wait for Jesus to come. As we read through the Old Testament, we see clues that should have helped people long ago know where, how and through whom the Savior would come. We get to read those old prophecies through the eyes of faith and with the benefit of knowing how it all turned out, but for the people of Mary's generation, and many who lived before her, the glory of God's promised salvation was obscured by misinterpretations and misplaced hopes in the wrong type of savior. They were waiting for God to save them, but they didn't yet understand how it would happen.

So, you can imagine how surprising the angel's words must have been for Mary. First, she would have been shocked that God had taken notice of her, a young woman from a small town pledged to be married to a man from an unremarkable family, despite their ancestral connection to King David 1,000 years before. Mary had no claim to fame or right to feel special above other young women of her time. The angel said she was "highly favored," which was a way of acknowledging the extraordinary grace of God that chose her for this special calling. Then, Mary had to take in the enormity of the task to which she was being called. She would give birth to a son, not Joseph's son, not a son conceived in the usual way of a husband and a wife, but the Son of the Most High. She would bear God's own Son, and He would be a king to reign forever over God's people.

None of us has ever been asked to do what Mary did. Her contribution to the Kingdom of God will always remain uniquely special. God asks us to do different work, but we share something vitally important with Mary: God invites us to play a role, however quiet or simple it may seem, in bringing to fulfillment the great promise of salvation. Many people still wait to meet the Savior. Some still don't realize that Jesus' birth is good news for them. We, who are highly favored by God and covered already by his abundant grace, can joyfully share the Christmas story and let the world know that the Savior has come.

Father in Heaven, thank You for sending Your Son into the world and for inviting people like Mary and like me to join in the work of Your Kingdom. Help me to serve You and to love others in my Savior's name. Amen.

Luke 1:34-38

"How will this be," Mary asked the angel, "since I am a virgin?"
The angel answered, "The Holy Spirit will come on you, and the power of the Most High will overshadow you. So the holy one to be born will be called the Son of God. Even Elizabeth your relative is going to have a child in her old age, and she who was said to be unable to conceive is in her sixth month. For no word from God will ever fail."

God doesn't concern himself with obstacles. He doesn't worry when the odds are stacked against him. He never gives up in the face of challenges or when people assume something is impossible. When God decides to do something, He does it, no matter what. When God makes a promise, He keeps his word, no matter how difficult it may seem. Mary was a virgin, and therefore, from a human perspective, from a biological standpoint, she could not conceive and give birth to a child. Mary understood this, and if we were in her shoes, we would have asked the same question she did: "How will this be?" So, the angel told Mary God's plan. The Holy Spirit will place the child in your womb, and He will be the Son of God.

The virgin birth has become a controversial, confusing and yet critical truth in the Christmas story. Some make Mary out to be an angel-like being who was chosen to bear the Christ-child because of her perfection. Others flatly reject this aspect of the story as an impossible myth. In faith, we read these words as profound and amazing truth. God did something miraculous through Mary, and the child she carried and gave birth to was not in fact her child, but God's own Son, a co-equal person of the Trinity, and God himself humbled into human form, from microscopic embryo to full-grown man who died on the cross. The virgin birth reminds us of God's miraculous power and of Jesus' divine nature. Mary was asked to believe the impossible and so are we, as we read the story of our Savior's birth.

The angel assured Mary, "For no word from God will ever fail." That's the assurance of our faith and the certainty of God's word. All that God says is true, and all his promises come to pass. When God tells us, "I will never leave you" (Hebrews 13:5), He means it. When the Spirit assures us that nothing "will be able to separate us from the love of God" (Romans 8:39), we know it's true. When Jesus promises, "I will come back and take you to be with me" (John 14:3), we can be sure of it. The Christmas story, from the angel's visit with Mary to the Child sleeping in the manger, proves that God always keeps his word. He always has and always will.

Thank You, Father, for Your faithfulness. You have made wonderful promises and fulfilled them all. Help me to walk in faith, trusting that You will do for me all that Your word says. I love You and pray in Jesus' name. Amen.

Luke 1:39-45

At that time Mary got ready and hurried to a town in the hill country of Judea, where she entered Zechariah's home and greeted Elizabeth. When Elizabeth heard Mary's greeting, the baby leaped in her womb, and Elizabeth was filled with the Holy Spirit. In a loud voice she exclaimed: "Blessed are you among women, and blessed is the child you will bear! But why am I so favored, that the mother of my Lord should come to me? As soon as the sound of your greeting reached my ears, the baby in my womb leaped for joy. Blessed is she who has believed that the Lord would fulfill his promises to her!"

When was the last time you leaped for joy? Maybe we should leave the leaping to younger people, but when was the last time you were so overcome with joy that you couldn't contain yourself? I suppose the birth of a child or the announcement of an engagement might inspire that sort of joy. Some of us may feel overwhelming happiness when our team wins a championship. There may be a few other examples of joy-kindling experiences in your life. What about your relationship with Jesus? When was the last time you were deeply moved by God's presence? It could happen during worship or prayer or as you read scripture and discover a new facet of God's grace.

This passage details two significant and touching encounters. First, Mary and Elizabeth greet one another, perhaps after not being together for a long time. They were relatives, perhaps aunt and niece or cousins once or twice removed. What they shared in common in this moment was not only their pregnancies but also faith in God's promises about their unborn children. Mary carried the Christ-child. Elizabeth carried, nearing full-term, John the Baptist. These two women were chosen to usher in the fulfillment of God's promise of salvation. The other extraordinary meeting was shared by the two infants, children whose bodies were still being knit together and yet whose souls already knew their purposes. John recognized the coming of the Savior and leaped for joy.

In many ways, our faith and devotion to Jesus mirror John the Baptist's ministry. He came to prepare the way for Jesus to enter people's lives, and in the same way, we also prepare people to meet the Savior as we share Jesus' love and message. John called people to repentance, preached God's word and then stepped aside so Jesus could take center stage. The ministry of the church follows that example, proclaiming truth and pointing people to Jesus, who alone can save the lost. We should also follow John's example of joy in the presence of the Savior. When we gather for worship or sit alone to pray, we should feel the joy of being near Jesus. When we read the Bible and hear God's voice speaking into our hearts, we should rejoice in his love and wisdom. When we feel the Spirit moving and witness his work in someone's life, we should celebrate God's grace. When we gather around the Christmas tree and the Advent wreath, we should be filled with the joy of knowing Jesus was born to save.

God of Grace and Glory, fill me anew with the joy of Your holy presence and the assurance of Your unending love. Make my joy overflow to others so they will be drawn to Jesus, in whose name I pray. Amen.

Luke 1:46-49

And Mary said:
"My soul glorifies the Lord
  and my spirit rejoices in God my Savior,
for he has been mindful
  of the humble state of his servant.
From now on all generations will call me blessed,
  for the Mighty One has done great things for me—
  holy is his name. …

We don't venerate Mary, consider her perfect, or for that matter, think she was any more or less human than anyone else. At the same time, we shouldn't shy away from admiring Mary for her deep faith, for her humble obedience and for the great blessing God bestowed on her. We should also respect Mary as one of the women God inspired to author a portion of the Bible. This young woman from a small town, probably with little education and no theological training, agreed to carry and raise the Christ-child and composed this song that has inspired millions of believers for 2,000 years. Mary deserves our admiration and should hold a special place in the hearts of believers, alongside the Disciples and the Apostle Paul, as one of the most influential followers of Jesus in the New Testament.

Admiration is not the same thing as adoration. We don't adore, worship or pray to Mary, and judging from the opening lines of her song, she didn't want anyone to. Mary understood just how blessed she was to be chosen as Jesus' mother, but her focus was not on her own saintliness. She was overwhelmed by the magnificence of God. Her soul glorified the Lord. Her spirit rejoiced in her Savior. She celebrated God as mighty and holy. Mary showed us how we should respond when God calls us to serve his good purposes. We don't boast in our greatness or push others aside to claim credit for what we achieve. We don't build a pedestal to display our own success. Instead, we glorify God for what He achieves through us, and we rejoice in the great things He does through our humble service.

The truth is, God has called you to serve in his Kingdom, just as He called Mary. Your calling will be different than Mary's, but you should feel just as blessed, just as honored to play a role in God's work of salvation. Some serve at home as loving parents and grandparents. Some serve at church in various ministries and administrative roles. Some serve in the mission fields of careers, neighborhoods and community involvement. Some serve publically, and some serve behind the scenes. There are numerous jobs in God's Kingdom and many ways we can share Jesus' love and message. May your spirit rejoice in the Savior and humbly join in service to his holy name.

Glorious Father, I rejoice in Your goodness, power and love. Thank You for calling me to serve You and for building Your church through the humble service of my sisters and brothers in Christ. Bless Your church and build Your kingdom, in Jesus' name. Amen.

Luke 1:50-51

His mercy extends to those who fear him,
from generation to generation.
He has performed mighty deeds with his arm;
he has scattered those who are proud in their inmost thoughts. ...

Christmas renews the promise of God's mercy. We could all use some mercy, couldn't we? In the midst of the hurts and illness and unrest of our world, God's mercy flows over us like cool, life-giving water. Jesus' birth was a gift of mercy. God saw our need, how lost and hopeless humanity was, caught in our own web of sin, blind in the darkness. He saw what we couldn't actually see ourselves: that without a Savior we would remain spiritually lost forever. God saw our need and had mercy on us. Jesus came with good news, died to pay for our sin, and rose again to open the door to heaven. The divine mercy that saves us also gives us hope for little, daily mercies along the way. The mercy of comfort through sorrow. The mercy of financial provision at the moment of need. The mercy of a fellow believer to listen and encourage. The mercy of friendship that breaks through loneliness.

God offers his mercy like a Christmas present, wrapped and waiting for us to accept. He extends mercy to "those who fear him," not forcing it on us, but holding it out through the message of Jesus, inviting those who desire God's goodness to receive it. We might wonder why anyone would reject God's love or walk away from the offer of new life in Christ, but the truth is, people say no to God all the time. One reason, as stated here, is human pride. Sometimes, we want to believe we don't need God. We are strong and smart and capable on our own, so why accept help from anyone, especially a God we can't see or touch? Pride tells us we don't need God's mercy. Those thoughts define the heart of an unbeliever, but sometimes, they also flow through my heart, and probably yours too.

Will you admit your need for God's mercy today? Will you confess that you are not strong enough or smart enough to carry your burdens? Will you stop trusting your own ideas and abilities long enough to pray for God's mercy to lift you up? It takes humility to receive mercy. We first have to say, "I am in need. I am lost. I am weak." Then we need to reach out and accept the gift of mercy God offers. The good news, made certain by Jesus' birth, is that our God delights in showing us mercy. He goes out of his way, even to the extent of being born as a little baby into our dark world, so He can offer mercy to people in need, like you and me.

Father, I need Your mercy. I am not able to carry my burdens or fix my problems without Your help. Thank You for seeing my need and offering to care for me with Your mighty arm. Teach me humility to accept Your mercy, through Jesus my Savior. Amen.

Luke 1:52-55

He has brought down rulers from their thrones
 but has lifted up the humble.
He has filled the hungry with good things
 but has sent the rich away empty.
He has helped his servant Israel,
 remembering to be merciful
to Abraham and his descendants forever,
 just as he promised our ancestors."

God has never been impressed with the power and wealth of people. We set up elaborate systems of authority, like our government and economic structures. We calculate financial fortunes and keep track of who owns the most of what we consider valuable. We honor rulers and tycoons, kings and moguls, presidents and chairmen of the board. Our worldly measures of success and power make it easy to tell who is on top and who is not. God, however, has never looked at people that way, and the Christmas story proves that He isn't impressed by earthly power.

Most of the world didn't even notice when Jesus was born. The King of Kings didn't arrive to fanfare or parades. He wasn't welcomed by dignitaries or heads of state. Jesus wasn't swaddled in silk or laid to sleep in a luxurious crib. Mary rightly understood, even before her child's birth, that God didn't intend to treat Jesus to the world's riches. God would rather lift up the humble and fill the hungry and be merciful to the faithful. Jesus' humble birth, like Mary's wise words, teach us who God is.

Maybe just as important, Mary's words should remind us who God wants us to be. It's so easy to join the world as they bow down to the powerful, the wealthy and the famous. We anxiously watch the stock market rise and fall, and we pin our hopes on elections and political promises. We envy celebrities, imagining the glamor of their seemingly perfect lives. We fall into all sorts of foolish traps set by the false promises of power and wealth. Meanwhile, Jesus points us to a better way. He invites us to humble devotion, faithful obedience and compassionate service. He asks us to trust in what God provides, believing that the good things He gives are better than what the world offers. The Christmas story invites us to fall out of love with the things of this world and to fall in love with Jesus, who came to satisfy the deepest longings of our hearts.

Gracious God, You give me what I need, even when I can't see my own emptiness or feel my own hunger. Thank You for filling me with good things. Teach me to seek after You and to join Jesus in showing mercy to people in need. I ask this in His good name. Amen.

Matthew 1:18-19

This is how the birth of Jesus the Messiah came about: His mother Mary was pledged to be married to Joseph, but before they came together, she was found to be pregnant through the Holy Spirit. Because Joseph her husband was faithful to the law, and yet did not want to expose her to public disgrace, he had in mind to divorce her quietly.

People these days tend to think that unwed mothers, infidelity and divorce are realities unique to our modern, permissive culture. We might be surprised to realize that people long ago dealt with moral failings and marriage problems. The Bible, in fact, has many references to these sorts of issues, including some of Jesus' own words about unfaithfulness and divorce. Now, I know what you're thinking: Mary's pregnancy was not the result of a moral failing and Joseph didn't actually divorce her. True enough. The situation later became clear to Joseph, who by faith accepted the truth about Mary's baby and where He came from. We also know that Mary's relative Elizabeth understood what a special gift from God Mary's baby was. And yet, it's still true that scripture records the fact that the circumstances surrounding Jesus' birth were clouded by suspicions of "public disgrace."

I often wonder why the Bible includes certain details while leaving others out. Wouldn't the Christmas story be simpler if we didn't have to think about Joseph questioning Mary's purity or considering an end to their engagement? We know it all worked out, but why would God want the story of our Savior's birth to include even a hint of impropriety or scandal? Maybe because it reminds us why Jesus was born. He came into our messy world to deal with our messy lives, and He wasn't afraid to let the mess of our sin fall on him. Jesus lived a sinless life, and his birth was a holy gift of God's love given through Mary's humble service. Jesus never did anything wrong, but his birth, his ministry and his death were all clouded by the messy suspicions and false accusations of our broken world. In the end, Jesus died on the cross to pay for it all and to wash us clean.

That's good news for us. We need to be reminded of it, because we are sinners. What people whispered about Mary and her Child may actually be true about you, me and people we know. The Bible records lots of sins committed by otherwise good, faithful people, like Abraham, David, Peter and Paul. We are all sinners, and we all need a Savior. That's why Jesus was born into our messy world and why his story includes all the messy details.

Father in Heaven, thank You for being honest about the realities of our world and about my need for a Savior. Forgive me for my sin, and help me to live in ways that obey Your word and honor the name of Jesus. Amen.

Matthew 1:20-21

But after he had considered this, an angel of the Lord appeared to him in a dream and said, "Joseph son of David, do not be afraid to take Mary home as your wife, because what is conceived in her is from the Holy Spirit. She will give birth to a son, and you are to give him the name Jesus, because he will save his people from their sins."

Names carry a great deal of theological weight in the Bible, like Adam naming the animals in the Garden, God changing Abraham's name, and Jesus calling Simon by the name Peter, "the Rock." In our culture, we tend to name children based on family traditions or the whims of popular culture, but in the Bible, names were meant to say something important about a person. From early in the Old Testament, we learn the mysterious significance of God's name, first spoken to Moses at the burning bush. God called himself "I Am Who I Am" (Exodus 3:14), which became the personal name of God, likely pronounced Yahweh and rendered in English Bibles as The Lord. As God prepared to send his Son into the world, He chose the name Jesus, most likely pronounced Yeshua, a variant of the Hebrew name we know as Joshua. The Hebrew meaning of his name is "The Lord is salvation" or "The Lord saves."

We also know Jesus as the Christ, as the Savior, as Immanuel, as the Lord, as the Son of God, and by many other names and titles given him in ancient prophecy and throughout the New Testament. Were we to name him according to all the extraordinary things He has done, we may never run out of titles: Miracle-worker, Healer, Water-walker, Storm-calmer, Teacher, Friend, Sin-Bearer, the Risen One. God chose Jesus, because of all the wonderful things He did while walking among us, offering salvation to sinners matters the most. Jesus' mission was to save us from our sins. Above all else, that's why He was born, that's why He came into our broken world, that's why He died on the cross, and that's why his resurrection gives us hope.

People celebrate Christmas for lots of reasons and in lots of different ways. For some it's just a fun season of presents, glittering trees and eggnog-flavored coffee. That's fine. At least, they are celebrating. For us, Christmas is the celebration of the Savior's birth. Jesus came into this world to save people from sin and death. We rejoice that God so loved the world that He sent his one and only Son so that all who believe in him shall not perish but have eternal life (John 3:16). His name is Jesus.

God of Grace, thank You for sending Jesus to save me from my sins. Give me opportunities to share His wonderful name with others so they can rejoice in the Savior's birth. I pray in Jesus' name. Amen.

Matthew 1:22-25

All this took place to fulfill what the Lord had said through the prophet: "The virgin will conceive and give birth to a son, and they will call him Immanuel" (which means "God with us").

When Joseph woke up, he did what the angel of the Lord had commanded him and took Mary home as his wife. But he did not consummate their marriage until she gave birth to a son. And he gave him the name Jesus.

Among the many hardships of the COVID pandemic, perhaps the most heartbreaking was how many people, particularly the elderly, were unable to visit loved ones, even in the final moments of life. Hospitals and care facilities severely restricted visitors, meaning in some cases that husbands and wives had to stay apart and children were not been able to visit parents or grandparents. Many people spent months alone, cut off from family and friends. Some died alone. The pandemic was cruel in many ways, as we longed for healing and the restoration of safe human contact. The Christmas story speaks to the longing we each have in our hearts to be near the ones we love. Jesus' incarnation touches the God-given desire for intimacy and face-to-face relationships that all humans share.

Jesus came as Immanuel. God came to be with us. He broke through the spiritual and earthly barriers between humanity and deity, being born among us so He could walk with us. Jesus not only came near to us, but He actually became one of us, participating fully in the whole range of human experience, from birth through death. It's one thing for God to know what we are like and to watch over the lives of people on earth, but through Immanuel, God chose to experience it all himself.

Now, Jesus' Spirit dwells within each of his followers, always with us, always near. The incarnation of Immanuel happened 2,000 years ago and lasted only three decades, but the promise of "God with us" remains true today and for eternity. You are never alone. Illness and quarantine can never separate you from God. The comforting presence of the Spirit abides with you through hardship. When you feel cut off from those you love, remember Immanuel. When you can't touch your family or dear friends, cling to the presence of the Spirit. When sorrow or fear or weariness weigh you down, find strength in the good news that Jesus came into this world to prove how deeply God loves you.

Good Father, thank You for sending Jesus into our world and for the abiding presence of Your Spirit in my heart. Give me the assurance that You are always with me, and help me to share the good news of Immanuel with those who feel alone or afraid. I ask this in Jesus' name. Amen.

Luke 2:1-7

In those days Caesar Augustus issued a decree that a census should be taken of the entire Roman world. (This was the first census that took place while Quirinius was governor of Syria.) And everyone went to their own town to register.

So Joseph also went up from the town of Nazareth in Galilee to Judea, to Bethlehem the town of David, because he belonged to the house and line of David. He went there to register with Mary, who was pledged to be married to him and was expecting a child. While they were there, the time came for the baby to be born, and she gave birth to her firstborn, a son. She wrapped him in cloths and placed him in a manger, because there was no guest room available for them.

This passage begins with the world's most powerful man and ends with the birth of a helpless child to a poor, forgotten family. Caesar Augustus, a tyrant with unquestioned authority and god-like status in the eyes of his subordinates, issued a decree that forced people all over the Roman world to interrupt their lives, travel far away, and give an accounting of their personal affairs. What took only the wave of the emperor's hand disrupted the lives of countless people like Mary and Joseph for weeks or months on end. Caesar didn't care that Mary was expecting a child. He wasn't concerned that no one would take them in for the night. The emperor couldn't care less about the tribulations of that little family who welcomed their firstborn in a stable instead of an inn, wrapped him in rough cloth instead of a fine gown, and placed him in a dirty feeding trough instead of a warm crib. Caesar and the principalities and powers of this world didn't even notice that Jesus was born that night.

Later in the story we'll hear about the choir of angels and the Magi bearing gifts for the newborn King, but for now we can't ignore the contrast between Caesar and the Christ-child, between the world's vainglory and the Savior's humility.

In the shadow of worldly power and prestige, many people feel unworthy and unnoticed. Jesus' humble birth, however, proves God cares for all people, no matter how insignificant or powerless we may seem in the eyes of the world. Jesus came to lift up the downtrodden, to give hope to the oppressed and to offer new life to those who know the sting of death. Jesus understands our struggles and hurts, our poverty and loneliness. He understands because He walked where we walk. He came not as a mighty ruler but as a lowly servant.

While we draw comfort from Jesus' humble birth and find hope in the surprising mercy of God on sinners like us, we also remember that Jesus is the King of Kings. His birth may have gone unnoticed by those sitting on earthly thrones, but Jesus came with the power of God and would soon show the world just how mighty and how merciful our God is. Caesar Augustus wielded authority for a few short years and enjoyed the fleeting luxuries of worldly riches. Jesus, while denying himself the comforts and glories of heaven, exercised the inexhaustible strength of God Almighty and remains our King and Savior forever.

Thank You, Father, for sending Jesus to be my King. Help me to honor Him in all I do and to trust in Your mercy and strength for all my needs. I pray in the name of the King of Kings. Amen.

Luke 2:8-14

And there were shepherds living out in the fields nearby, keeping watch over their flocks at night. An angel of the Lord appeared to them, and the glory of the Lord shone around them, and they were terrified. But the angel said to them, "Do not be afraid. I bring you good news that will cause great joy for all the people. Today in the town of David a Savior has been born to you; he is the Messiah, the Lord. This will be a sign to you: You will find a baby wrapped in cloths and lying in a manger."

Suddenly a great company of the heavenly host appeared with the angel, praising God and saying,

"Glory to God in the highest heaven,
and on earth peace to those on whom his favor rests."

Do not be afraid. What a wonderful and timely message for our world. As people have done throughout history, we tend to focus on today's bad news or fret over the latest reason for fear. We imagine that our present struggles must be worse than what people before us had to endure. We look up, like the shepherds did, and are terrified by what we see. The truth is, there are many things in this world to be afraid of. There are wars, pandemics, famines, natural disasters, crime and domestic violence. We do bad things, and we have bad things done to us. All the bad things we see and hear send shivers down our spines and fill our hearts with fear, but God sends us a message of peace: Do not be afraid.

Of course, what the shepherds saw in the sky that night was not intended to cause fear. They didn't understand at first, but they were witnesses to an extraordinary manifestation of God's glory. First there appeared one angel, perhaps Gabriel who had visited both Mary and Zechariah, and then a large choir of angels appeared in the sky. The great company of angels is called a "host," which can also be translated as an army. This heavenly army did not come to wage war but to offer peace. Angels are God's messengers, whose appearance may frighten people even as they deliver messages of hope, peace and grace. The shepherds were stunned by the glorious sight they saw and amazed by the comforting words they heard.

We need to hear the angel's message anew: Do not be afraid. Yes, this world is filled with trouble and hardship. Yes, we will face more challenges tomorrow and may have to endure scary moments in the days ahead. Jesus even told us, "In this world you will have trouble," and we know He was telling the truth. Then He added words of hope and peace: "But take heart! I have overcome the world" (John 16:33). So, do not be afraid. You are not alone. God watches over you. His heavenly army stands ready to protect you. He sent Jesus to give us peace, and that peace overcomes the fear.

Glorious Lord, take away my fear and give me Your peace. Teach me to trust in You, so I can overcome the world's trouble through faith in Jesus. I love You and rejoice in the good news of my Savior. Amen.

Luke 2:15-21

When the angels had left them and gone into heaven, the shepherds said to one another, "Let's go to Bethlehem and see this thing that has happened, which the Lord has told us about."

So they hurried off and found Mary and Joseph, and the baby, who was lying in the manger. When they had seen him, they spread the word concerning what had been told them about this child, and all who heard it were amazed at what the shepherds said to them. But Mary treasured up all these things and pondered them in her heart. The shepherds returned, glorifying and praising God for all the things they had heard and seen, which were just as they had been told.

On the eighth day, when it was time to circumcise the child, he was named Jesus, the name the angel had given him before he was conceived.

As a child, no moment in the year could hold a candle to Christmas morning. In my boyhood home, the elves would busy themselves as soon as my brother and I went to bed. Mom and Dad would arrange the gifts, some wrapped under the tree, some stuffed into stockings hung merrily from the mantel. In the magical morning, I would wake with one thought in my mind, echoing the shepherd's excitement: "Let's go and see this thing that has happened!" For me, the thing was Christmas presents and a day of happiness. For the shepherds, it was the true reason for joy at Christmas. They didn't run off to a decorated tree surrounded by gifts. They hurried to find the baby born to save the world.

I hope the excitement and joy of Christmas has not faded too much from your heart through the years. Kids know how to enjoy Christmas, with all its wonder and fun. As adults, we may let the season's busyness and life's stressfulness get in the way of rejoicing in our Savior's birth. Remember the shepherds, hurrying off to Bethlehem. Remember the amazement of those who heard their story. Remember Mary who treasured up in her heart all that had happened. Our joy on Christmas morning shouldn't just come from gifts or decorations or special meals shared with loved ones. Those things are nice, but they point to something far, far better. They remind us what the shepherds hurried off to see.

They found Mary, Joseph and the newborn child, lying in a manger. They found God's great gift of grace. They found the fulfillment of a multitude of prophecies and promises. They found the King and the Savior. We have found the Savior too, and He is the reason we rejoice at Christmas. May God bless you this day, and may you share with those you love the good news of Jesus.

God of Love, thank You for sending Jesus to be my Savior and for filling my heart with joy. Send me, like the shepherds who spread the word about Jesus' birth, to share Your love and message with people in need. I pray in the name of Jesus my Savior. Amen.

THE SERMON ON THE MOUNT

Jesus taught God's wisdom. Crowds gathered to hear him, sometimes listening to him preach and tell stories all day long. He spoke with authority and often challenged his listeners to change their ways and renew their hearts. The Sermon on the Mount, recorded in Matthew 5-7, invites us to follow the wisdom of God instead of the ways of this world. Some of Jesus' words may make us uncomfortable, and some may sound impossible to follow. All of Jesus' words invite us to live the way He lived. May you grow to become more like Jesus in word, action, thought, attitude and love for God.

Matthew 5:1-5

Now when Jesus saw the crowds, he went up on a mountainside and sat down. His disciples came to him, and he began to teach them.
He said:
"Blessed are the poor in spirit,
*   for theirs is the kingdom of heaven.*
Blessed are those who mourn,
*   for they will be comforted.*
Blessed are the meek,
*   for they will inherit the earth.*

We all like blessings, especially when life has been hard or after we have been denied things we usually take for granted. We long for happy, pleasant things. I'm sure you could use a nice package full of blessings about now. Jesus understands that, and He wants to bring us comfort and joy. In fact, Jesus wants to bless us even during the trials and hardships of life, and that's really the beauty of the blessings Jesus promises. They don't come in the form of pleasure and luxury; instead, Jesus invites us to find a new kind of blessing that we can enjoy even if we are poor in spirit, even while we mourn, and even as we treat others in meek, gentle ways.

The people Jesus preached to on that mountainside knew all about hardship. They struggled each day just to survive. They endured harsh treatment from local authorities and abuse from Roman soldiers. They grew up learning an unforgiving form of religion that made God into a demanding overlord. They knew all about being poor in spirit, having hearts filled with sorrow and hopelessness. Jesus told them that God wanted to give them a far better life, a life overflowing with blessings that transcend the hardships of this world.

We often walk down hard roads and mourn the loss of people and things we love. Life can be rough and often is. But the promises of God invite us to see beyond material need or abundance, beyond the immediate circumstances of today, and to find comfort in God's love. Jesus gives us the hope of heaven, the comfort of the Spirit's presence, and the assurance that this world still belongs to God and we still belong to Him.

Thank You, Jesus, for speaking truth and hope into my life. Help me to receive the blessings You give and to rejoice in Your everlasting love. Amen.

Matthew 5:6-12

Blessed are those who hunger and thirst for righteousness,
 for they will be filled.
Blessed are the merciful,
 for they will be shown mercy.
Blessed are the pure in heart,
 for they will see God.
Blessed are the peacemakers,
 for they will be called children of God.
Blessed are those who are persecuted because of righteousness,
 for theirs is the kingdom of heaven.
Blessed are you when people insult you, persecute you and falsely say all kinds of evil against you because of me. Rejoice and be glad, because great is your reward in heaven, for in the same way they persecuted the prophets who were before you.

What do you hunger and thirst for? Some people may answer: money or happiness or personal freedoms or good health. Jesus blesses those who most deeply desire righteousness, that state of being in our lives and in the world around us that reflects God's values and truth. What do you make? Some people say they make things like: money or trouble or their own good luck. Jesus blesses those who make peace, who draw people together in unity, who treat others with kindness and love in order to soften their hearts.

Jesus blesses people who live and act the way He did. Jesus was meek, merciful and pure in heart. He made peace and hungered for righteousness. He blessed others and called them to be a blessing too. Jesus was also "persecuted because of righteousness," and He told his followers to prepare themselves to face insults and false accusations. The world often rejects the things of God, often ridicules those who obey God, and often curses what God blesses.

This passage, known as the Beatitudes (blessings),

introduces the Sermon on the Mount, in which Jesus told his followers about life in the Kingdom of God. He was about to ask them to live in ways the world wouldn't understand and to be willing to suffer for the sake of honoring God. Jesus knew his followers would face some tough moments, and that's why He began the sermon with words of blessing. We need to hear these words too and remember that Jesus blesses us in ways and for reasons the world doesn't understand. We choose to hunger for righteousness and to make peace. We choose to be merciful and pure. Some people may not understand why we act this way, but Jesus blesses us for it.

Father in heaven, You are righteous, merciful and holy. Thank You for blessing me through Jesus my Savior. Help me to become more like Him in all I do. Amen.

Matthew 5:13-16

You are the salt of the earth. But if the salt loses its saltiness, how can it be made salty again? It is no longer good for anything, except to be thrown out and trampled underfoot.

You are the light of the world. A town built on a hill cannot be hidden. Neither do people light a lamp and put it under a bowl. Instead they put it on its stand, and it gives light to everyone in the house. In the same way, let your light shine before others, that they may see your good deeds and glorify your Father in heaven.

I love a big bowl of salty popcorn. And briny pickles on my hamburger. I don't think I'm alone in being a big fan of salt. It makes food taste better. It brightens up otherwise dull flavors. Even vegetables can taste good with a little sprinkle of salt! And light? I love a bright sunrise on a clear morning. A flashlight to shine underneath the couch when looking for a lost coin is invaluable. Light makes our world better, doesn't it? Jesus knew what He was talking about, as usual. These verses are often dissected to the point of meaninglessness, with weird explanations of obscure uses for salt and speculation about the design of lamps in Jesus' time. Those musings might fill a few pages in a Bible commentary, but we can all understand Jesus' words just the way He said them: salt and light are good.

We live in a world filled with unpleasant things. We often have to eat flavorless meals and walk through dark rooms. We suffer from illness and anxiety. We stumble ahead without knowing which is the right way to take. We endure long periods of waiting and worrying. We seek guidance from worldly wisdom only to discover we are being led along by someone just as blind as we are. This world longs for salt and light.

Jesus asks us to give the world what it so desperately needs. He calls us to love people in his name and to tell them good news. Jesus asks us to bring cups of cold water to those who thirst and to speak God's truth to those who are lost. Jesus invites us to join him in sprinkling the salt of hope and joy over hearts bored by flavorless life. He invites us to shine the light of his goodness, mercy and grace into dark corners where people feel helpless and hopeless. Salt and light make the world better, and Jesus wants us to share them with people in need.

Gracious Lord, You give good things to those You love. You make my life better. Show me how I can share Your love with people I know and how I can spread hope in the name of Jesus, through whom I pray. Amen.

Matthew 5:17-20

Do not think that I have come to abolish the Law or the Prophets; I have not come to abolish them but to fulfill them. For truly I tell you, until heaven and earth disappear, not the smallest letter, not the least stroke of a pen, will by any means disappear from the Law until everything is accomplished. Therefore anyone who sets aside one of the least of these commands and teaches others accordingly will be called least in the kingdom of heaven, but whoever practices and teaches these commands will be called great in the kingdom of heaven. For I tell you that unless your righteousness surpasses that of the Pharisees and the teachers of the law, you will certainly not enter the kingdom of heaven.

We all resist following the rules. It's the nature of sin in our hearts. We resent being told what to do and being held accountable for the ways we break the rules. We might know the rules are for our own good and for the sake of protecting others. We might fully appreciate the benefits of doing what is right and helpful, but there's still part of us, especially as freedom-loving Americans, that doesn't like being told what we can and can't do.

"The Law" Jesus referred to is recorded in the Pentateuch, the first five books of the Bible. "The Prophets" brings in much of the rest of the Old Testament. Of course, the New Testament had not yet been written, so in a shorthand way, Jesus was saying that we must obey all of scripture. We don't get to pick and choose the parts we like and the parts we will just ignore. Obedience and righteousness don't work that way. All of God's word, even the hard parts, reveal who God is and how He wants us to live. Jesus came to fulfill it all, to be the one perfectly obedient follower of God's word.

At the same time, Jesus knew we would fall short of his standard of perfection, and while He doesn't let us off the hook in terms of what God expects from us, Jesus came into this world to deal with our imperfection, with our sinfulness, with all the ways we resist following the rules. Jesus came to die for our sin and set us free. Freedom in Christ doesn't give us license to break more rules. It gives us grace to get back up and try again to be righteous and good, knowing that we are forgiven by a loving God, not condemned by a vengeful one. The good news of Jesus is that through His death and resurrection, God declares us righteous, perfect and pure in his sight.

Gracious Father, thank You for sending Jesus to die for my sins and to offer me eternal life. Forgive me for breaking Your rules. Help me to honor You in all I do and to love others in Jesus' name. I ask this through my Savior. Amen.

Matthew 5:21-26

You have heard that it was said to the people long ago, "You shall not murder, and anyone who murders will be subject to judgment." But I tell you that anyone who is angry with a brother or sister will be subject to judgment. Again, anyone who says to a brother or sister, "Raca," is answerable to the court. And anyone who says, "You fool!" will be in danger of the fire of hell.

Therefore, if you are offering your gift at the altar and there remember that your brother or sister has something against you, leave your gift there in front of the altar. First go and be reconciled to them; then come and offer your gift.

Settle matters quickly with your adversary who is taking you to court. Do it while you are still together on the way, or your adversary may hand you over to the judge, and the judge may hand you over to the officer, and you may be thrown into prison. Truly I tell you, you will not get out until you have paid the last penny.

It is heartbreaking to see how our nation has been torn asunder by political and cultural divisions, characterized by outrage mixed with a strong dose of actual rage. We witness this anger simmering under the surface of our public discourse. Some people, especially those who earn their living talking on television and posting on social media, love to hate, and they don't seem the least bit ashamed of their rage-filled words. It might be tempting for us to pass judgment on those talking heads, but we should be careful, because Jesus' words are also about our words. I would never commit murder, but I have called someone a fool, and I have cursed people under my breath or in the dark corners of my mind.

Remember, Jesus had just said that our righteousness must exceed that of the Pharisees, those religious do-gooders who painstakingly obeyed every tiny legal statute but whose hearts were cold in the presence of God. Jesus wants us to know that what happens in our hearts, the words we speak and the thoughts that linger in our minds say as much about our state of righteousness as do actual acts of violence or sexual sin. The same goes for grudges we hold and disputes we choose not to settle. God sees and hears it all.

Jesus cares about how you treat other people, especially people who think, act, look, speak and live differently than you do. That's the real test, isn't it? How will I treat someone with whom I disagree? What will I say to the person who offends me? Will I be a peacemaker or a quarreler? We hear "Raca" everywhere in our culture. To calm the rage and quiet the conflicts, Jesus asks us to speak "peace," "love," "hope" and "good news."

Father of Peace, help me to share Your love with others and to bring peace into Your world, in place of anger and strife. Use me to speak words of hope in Jesus' name. Amen.

Matthew 5:27-32

You have heard that it was said, "You shall not commit adultery." But I tell you that anyone who looks at a woman lustfully has already committed adultery with her in his heart. If your right eye causes you to stumble, gouge it out and throw it away. It is better for you to lose one part of your body than for your whole body to be thrown into hell. And if your right hand causes you to stumble, cut it off and throw it away. It is better for you to lose one part of your body than for your whole body to go into hell.

It has been said, "Anyone who divorces his wife must give her a certificate of divorce." But I tell you that anyone who divorces his wife, except for sexual immorality, makes her the victim of adultery, and anyone who marries a divorced woman commits adultery.

Jesus never shied away from sensitive subjects. It must have been shocking in his day for a rabbi to openly discuss private matters like sex and marital fidelity. Yes, the Old Testament law has many references to sexual sin and sets clear standards for marriage and personal purity, but people have always felt a degree of shame when confronted about things we do in private. The truth is, we know Jesus' words are directed at us, at all of us.

Jesus addresses here several serious issues, particularly sexual sins that bring devastating damage to families and communities. Every sin has consequences, and that is particularly true with sexual sin. We hurt others and ourselves when we violate God's standards, even when the sin happens in our thoughts. Jesus reminds us that nothing we do is hidden from God, and righteousness requires integrity, a God-honoring way of life that is consistent through and through. We need to be the same person of faith, compassion and love in private, behind closed doors, even in the quiet of our minds, as we act like we are in front of other people.

Honoring God and following Jesus is not a spectator

sport. We don't act good just to look good to other people. We don't treat our spouse well or love our kids just so our neighbors will think well of us. Jesus calls us to be better than that kind of hypocrisy and disingenuous pretense. Jesus calls us to be righteous, inside and out. When we fall short, He offers us grace, calls us to repent and asks us to do better the next time.

Thank You, Jesus, for speaking hard truths and for calling me to follow You in every part of my life. Forgive me for all my sins, and help me to grow in purity of thought and integrity of action, so I can spread the light of Your goodness to those around me. Amen.

Matthew 5:33-37

Again, you have heard that it was said to the people long ago, "Do not break your oath, but fulfill to the Lord the vows you have made." But I tell you, do not swear an oath at all: either by heaven, for it is God's throne; or by the earth, for it is his footstool; or by Jerusalem, for it is the city of the Great King. And do not swear by your head, for you cannot make even one hair white or black. All you need to say is simply "Yes" or "No"; anything beyond this comes from the evil one.

Of all the serious and difficult things Jesus taught, this passage may not strike us as ranking very high on the list. It's not as startling as do not lust. It's not as surprising as love your enemies. It's not as memorable as love your neighbor as yourself. But in many ways, this wisdom about simply saying yes or no is just what our culture needs to hear. We swim in a sea of outrageous rhetoric, outlandish claims and half-truths masquerading as gospel. Whether it's called fake news or clickbait or just good old-fashioned lies, people will say anything to grab our attention or to bash the opposition. The more extreme, the better. The more insulting, the more interesting. The more shocking, the more views and comments and re-tweets. Those are the rules of engagement in social media, and all too often, they are applied in real life relationships too.

Jesus told us not to mince our words or to exaggerate their meaning. You don't need to swear by heaven or earth or (for some reason) your own head. Just say yes or no. You don't need to make a big show of your opinions and your ideas. Just speak plainly. In other words, tell the truth, simple and honest, and that will be enough.

How refreshing it would be if politicians, advertisers and media personalities would just tell us clearly what we need to know, without the hype and innuendo. Maybe we could start believing what they tell us. We all know we can't control what others say, but we can take ownership of our own tongues. We can choose to speak truth. We can choose to say a few good, honest words instead of many, deceitful words. We can say yes or no, and leave it at that.

Gracious Lord, thank You for telling me the truth. Forgive me for all my useless, foolish, untrue words. Help me to speak clearly and honestly, all the time. I pray that my example of speaking the truth would draw others toward Jesus, in whose name I pray. Amen.

Matthew 5:38-48

You have heard that it was said, 'Eye for eye, and tooth for tooth.' But I tell you, do not resist an evil person. If anyone slaps you on the right cheek, turn to them the other cheek also. And if anyone wants to sue you and take your shirt, hand over your coat as well. If anyone forces you to go one mile, go with them two miles. Give to the one who asks you, and do not turn away from the one who wants to borrow from you.

You have heard that it was said, 'Love your neighbor and hate your enemy.' But I tell you, love your enemies and pray for those who persecute you, that you may be children of your Father in heaven. He causes his sun to rise on the evil and the good, and sends rain on the righteous and the unrighteous. If you love those who love you, what reward will you get? Are not even the tax collectors doing that? And if you greet only your own people, what are you doing more than others? Do not even pagans do that? Be perfect, therefore, as your heavenly Father is perfect.

Most of us like to help people in need, especially a family member or a friend who we know is facing a tough moment. We like to be generous and kind. It makes us feel good inside to do something helpful. That's why we like these words that Jesus spoke. On the surface, we like the idea of loving our neighbors and giving to someone in need, and we even feel noble when we get to turn the other cheek. Be careful, though, about digging deeper into what Jesus said here. Are we really ready to love people who actively oppose us? Are we really happy to settle a dispute by giving the other person more than they wanted in the first place? Do we really feel good inside when God blesses the unrighteous?

Jesus asks a lot of us. He sets the standard for how we are supposed to behave and treat others so high that the only word sufficient for it is "perfect." Anything less than perfection is falling short. So, it's not enough to love those who love us or to be generous only to our friends and family. No, Jesus asks us to love those who oppose us and to go the extra mile in service to anyone in need.

We see opportunities everywhere to live out Jesus' words. There are people in need all around us, and there are demanding, hard-to-love people around every corner. Faithfully and joyfully following Jesus by loving difficult people is how we shine light into darkness, how we bring salt to a flavorless, dying world. When we choose to love in ways that don't come naturally, we show others who Jesus is and how much He has changed our hearts.

Thank You, Father, for sending Jesus to show me the way of love. Forgive me for only loving some people, some of the time. Help me to go the extra mile to care for those You call me to love, in Jesus' name. Amen.

Matthew 6:1-4

Be careful not to practice your righteousness in front of others to be seen by them. If you do, you will have no reward from your Father in heaven.

So when you give to the needy, do not announce it with trumpets, as the hypocrites do in the synagogues and on the streets, to be honored by others. Truly I tell you, they have received their reward in full. But when you give to the needy, do not let your left hand know what your right hand is doing, so that your giving may be in secret. Then your Father, who sees what is done in secret, will reward you.

From my observation of human behavior, it's easy to see that most people like to keep their financial status and decisions as private as possible. We use passwords, PINs, safes and super-sophisticated encryption algorithms to keep other people from knowing anything about our money. Except when it comes to making donations. Then people post about their generosity on social media, brag about it to neighbors and friends, and sometimes, if the amount they give is really impressive, insist that their name be emblazoned on the object or building they made possible through their magnanimity.

Jesus cautioned us against seeking human accolades for our acts of generosity. It's great to be generous. God smiles on our giving and is pleased when we bless others. Just don't do it in a way that brings honor to yourself. In God's economy, the motivation behind a good deed or a generous gift determines its value. A little donation given secretly and cheerfully matters more in God's Kingdom than a big contribution given for the good of the giver. God judges our hearts along with our actions.

So, when you give or serve those in need or feel inspired to be kind to a neighbor, do it joyfully, and as best you can, do it without bringing attention to yourself. Give to bring glory to God. Share what you have in the name of Jesus. Then, you can expect Jesus' promise of blessing to flow back to you and enable you to be generous again and again.

Father in Heaven, thank You for being generous in how You love me. Help me to share with others what You have given me and to trust that You will continue to meet my needs. I pray this through Jesus, who gave Himself for me. Amen.

Matthew 6:5-8

And when you pray, do not be like the hypocrites, for they love to pray standing in the synagogues and on the street corners to be seen by others. Truly I tell you, they have received their reward in full. But when you pray, go into your room, close the door and pray to your Father, who is unseen. Then your Father, who sees what is done in secret, will reward you. And when you pray, do not keep on babbling like pagans, for they think they will be heard because of their many words. Do not be like them, for your Father knows what you need before you ask him.

There was a lot of talk during 2020 about how and when to "re-open" churches, along with re-opening restaurants, hair salons and other businesses in the wake of the pandemic. While these were important conversations as the world slowly emerged from quarantine, I can assure you that the church was never closed. Yes, our building was much quieter than normal for a time, and no, we didn't worshiping all together on Sunday mornings for several weeks. But ministry continued, as did worship and fellowship. And prayer? My guess is, prayer greatly increased.

Jesus wants us to know that prayer doesn't have to happen in a synagogue or on a street corner or inside a church sanctuary. In fact, Jesus asks us to pray at home, in quiet corners where only God can hear our prayers. Of course, we can also pray in public and in church, but when we do, we need to be careful not to turn a public prayer into a performance with a spotlight shining on the person at the microphone. That's not the right spirit for prayer. Jesus said prayer should be quiet, simple and honest.

You can pray right now, right where you are, just as powerfully and effectively as I can pray during worship on a Sunday morning in front of our whole church family. God hears a short, heart-felt prayer whispered in the stillness of your bedroom, just as clearly as He hears a prayer amplified through a grand cathedral. Jesus promised that's true. So, lift up your prayers with faith wherever you are, knowing that God sees into your heart and knows all your needs.

Thank You, Jesus, for teaching me to pray. Thank You for hearing me and promising that my prayers are powerful in Your name. Remind me to pray often for the people You love. Teach me and everyone to trust in You. I pray this in Jesus' name. Amen.

Matthew 6:9-15

This, then, is how you should pray:
"Our Father in heaven,
hallowed be your name,
your kingdom come,
your will be done,
   on earth as it is in heaven.
Give us today our daily bread.
And forgive us our debts,
   as we also have forgiven our debtors.
And lead us not into temptation,
   but deliver us from the evil one."
For if you forgive other people when they sin against you, your heavenly Father will also forgive you. But if you do not forgive others their sins, your Father will not forgive your sins.

How do you pray? Who taught you how to pray? I guess the best answer to both questions is to say that we pray like Jesus because He taught us how. Even if that isn't entirely true in your life, we can always relearn how to pray from Jesus. The format for effective prayer Jesus gives us here contains quite a few surprises that may show us we don't always pray the way we should. For example, Jesus' prayer focuses on God, not us or the long list of requests and concerns we often bring to our times of prayer.

That's why Jesus teaches us to pray for God's kingdom to come and for his will to be done. I don't always pray like that. Instead, I often pray that God would give me what I want. Jesus also says we should pray for daily bread, which means I have to submit to what God wants to give me today and then trust that He will give a little more tomorrow. I would prefer to have enough to last a good long time, but Jesus wants me to trust God every day. Even when we pray for forgiveness, Jesus tells us to turn the focus away from our own needs and toward the needs of others, just as He gave his life for ours.

Learning to pray begins with learning to love and submit to God. Too often, we turn prayer into a list of wants and needs. Jesus calls us to seek after what God wants, to trust that his will really is better than my will and that what God desires to give me will be a greater blessing than what I may desire for myself. Praying Jesus' way takes faith, courage and humility.

Father in heaven, You are holy. May Your perfect will rule over my life and over this world. Give me what I need, and help me to live a life that honors Jesus, in whose name I pray. Amen.

Matthew 6:16-18

When you fast, do not look somber as the hypocrites do, for they disfigure their faces to show others they are fasting. Truly I tell you, they have received their reward in full. But when you fast, put oil on your head and wash your face, so that it will not be obvious to others that you are fasting, but only to your Father, who is unseen; and your Father, who sees what is done in secret, will reward you.

  I'm noticing a pattern here. First, we should give without letting others know about it. Then, we should pray in private where only God can hear. Now, Jesus tells us to fast without bringing attention to ourselves. And remember what He said about lusting in your heart and hating someone in your mind? It turns out that God cares about what happens in our hearts, about our motivations and attitudes, and that He is not fooled by insincere religious gestures or shallow acts of devotion. When you fast, do it only for God to see.

  That's not how the Pharisees fasted or practiced their form of religion. They put on a big show, making sure that everyone could see and hear just how religious and righteous they were. More like self-righteous. Jesus saw right through their pretense and vanity. Just as you can't worship two things at once (like God and yourself), you can't fast for two purposes (to honor God and to make yourself look good). The second purpose negates the first, and your fasting or worship becomes meaningless.

  Fasting is a form of prayer. It's a way of removing distractions and temptations so you can focus your heart more fully on God. Fasting is also hard. If you fast from food, you will feel hungry. If you fast from technology, you will feel out of touch. If you fast from a favorite hobby or activity, you will feel deprived. Fasting teaches us to turn to God in the midst of need, to trust that He alone is sufficient to truly satisfy us. This type of devotional experience should be kept just between you and God, as you submit your heart and receive the blessing of God's faithful mercy.

Gracious Father, teach me to submit fully to Your will. Give me times of quiet and peace to sit in Your holy presence and to know Your unending love. Fill my heart more fully with Your Spirit. I pray this in Jesus' name. Amen.

Matthew 6:19-24

Do not store up for yourselves treasures on earth, where moths and vermin destroy, and where thieves break in and steal. But store up for yourselves treasures in heaven, where moths and vermin do not destroy, and where thieves do not break in and steal. For where your treasure is, there your heart will be also.

The eye is the lamp of the body. If your eyes are healthy, your whole body will be full of light. But if your eyes are unhealthy, your whole body will be full of darkness. If then the light within you is darkness, how great is that darkness!

No one can serve two masters. Either you will hate the one and love the other, or you will be devoted to the one and despise the other. You cannot serve both God and money.

Where do you keep your treasure? By the way, that's a different question than asking, "What is your treasure?" If you keep your treasure in the bank or in the stock market or hidden in a lockbox under your bed, then I could probably guess what kind of treasure you have. I could also tell you, along with Jesus, the many ways your treasure could be lost or taken away from you. Money may make the world go round, but it can never leave this world. On the other hand, if you keep your treasure in heaven, then you have something to look forward to that will last forever and ever.

The truth is, Jesus had a complicated relationship with money, and so do we. Jesus understood the need to use money to buy food and to care for people in need. His ministry received support from wealthy donors. He urged his followers to pay taxes and to give to worthy causes. At the same time, Jesus knew that money can become a master over us, enslaving us with greed, envy, worry and faithless self-reliance. In the end, we can't serve God effectively and faithfully while our hearts long after wealth.

So much in this world is judged on a financial scale.

Our worth is too often measured by what our investments are worth. But that's not how God looks at you. He doesn't love you because of what you own or what you owe. He loves you according to his grace poured out through Jesus Christ. That's why you need to set your heart on the treasure of heaven, to long after what only God can give you and what the world can never take away. Through faith, you belong to Jesus, and by God's grace you always and forever will. That's your real treasure, and it's worth more than all the wealth of this world.

Gracious Father, You are the treasure my heart longs for. Forgive me for allowing money and things to master me. Help me to honor You with how I use the resources You allow me to have in this life and to remember that what waits for me in heaven will be so much better. I ask this through Jesus, my true Master. Amen.

Matthew 6:25-34

Therefore I tell you, do not worry about your life, what you will eat or drink; or about your body, what you will wear. Is not life more than food, and the body more than clothes? Look at the birds of the air; they do not sow or reap or store away in barns, and yet your heavenly Father feeds them. Are you not much more valuable than they? Can any one of you by worrying add a single hour to your life?

And why do you worry about clothes? See how the flowers of the field grow. They do not labor or spin. Yet I tell you that not even Solomon in all his splendor was dressed like one of these. If that is how God clothes the grass of the field, which is here today and tomorrow is thrown into the fire, will he not much more clothe you—you of little faith? So do not worry, saying, 'What shall we eat?' or 'What shall we drink?' or 'What shall we wear?' For the pagans run after all these things, and your heavenly Father knows that you need them. But seek first his kingdom and his righteousness, and all these things will be given to you as well. Therefore do not worry about tomorrow, for tomorrow will worry about itself. Each day has enough trouble of its own.

I come from a long line of worriers. I don't know if it's a genetic trait or a learned behavior, but I'm pretty sure most of us are better at worrying than we are at being patient or trusting God or feeling content. We worry about everything, from basic needs like clothes and food, to things that don't even really affect our lives like what other people might think about us. We worry about big things like wars, pandemics and the collapse of society, and about little things like what if it rains the day after I wash my car.

Jesus pointed us to the birds and the flowers to remind us that we humans, for all our intelligence and ingenuity, often over-think life. Birds don't calculate exactly how many seeds they should eat today so there will be enough left for tomorrow and the day after that. Flowers don't stand in front of a mirror wondering what someone else will think about their new shoes and hairstyle. Instead, they simply live as God created them and accept what God provides. Wouldn't it be nice to live like a bird for a while?

Well, maybe you can, at least in some ways. Remember that God created you and loves you. He knows just what you need. He sees what you are facing today and knows what tomorrow will bring. Remember that God has plenty of blessings ready for you, so long as you are willing to wait patiently and gratefully for each one. The more you remember God's goodness and grace, the more you will forget all your worries. Life is better that way.

Thank You, Jesus, for reminding me how much You love me. Teach me to trust You each day, for all that I need, and show me how I can bring hope and encouragement to others. Thank You for hearing my prayers, in Jesus' name. Amen.

Matthew 7:1-6

Do not judge, or you too will be judged. For in the same way you judge others, you will be judged, and with the measure you use, it will be measured to you.

Why do you look at the speck of sawdust in your brother's eye and pay no attention to the plank in your own eye? How can you say to your brother, 'Let me take the speck out of your eye,' when all the time there is a plank in your own eye? You hypocrite, first take the plank out of your own eye, and then you will see clearly to remove the speck from your brother's eye.

Do not give dogs what is sacred; do not throw your pearls to pigs. If you do, they may trample them under their feet, and turn and tear you to pieces.

Our culture has been mired in the muck of hypocrisy and moralistic judgmentalism for years, and perhaps never more so than during election years. Each side takes their side of each issue and clings to their moral high ground for dear life while casting stones and calling for retribution against anyone who dares contradict their sacred opinions. Has a culture ever been this divided before? Have people ever been so hypocritically judgmental? Well, judging from Jesus' words, yes, people have struggled with these same failings for at least the last 2,000 years. Passing judgment on others is nothing new. Criticizing someone else for doing the very thing you are doing has been around for a long time. Jesus saw it in the 1st Century and knew we would deal with it too.

Truth is, hypocrisy is not just a cultural problem or a byproduct of our cynical political system. Each one of us, in our private thoughts and public words, passes judgment and calls out the sins of our neighbors while committing similar sins ourselves. You remember what Jesus said when confronted about the woman caught in adultery: "Let any one of you who is without sin be the first to throw a stone" (John

8:7). None of us is in a position to throw stones.

Instead, we need to repent of our own sins and hypocritical behavior. We need to put our hearts right, and then we will be in a better position to encourage others to repent as well. And if we feel the need to gently, humbly call a friend to repentance, we need to speak truth in love, seeking good for our friend, not heaping shame on them. With all the problems and divisions in our world today, it's tough to follow Jesus' words. It's hard to be a peacemaker and an encourager of the good. But that's certainly what our world needs, isn't it?

Holy Father, You are perfect and pure. Forgive me for all my sins, including the hypocritical ways I treat others. Show me how to love people the way You do and how to live in ways that honor the name of Jesus, through whom I pray. Amen.

Matthew 7:7-8

Ask and it will be given to you; seek and you will find; knock and the door will be opened to you. For everyone who asks receives; the one who seeks finds; and to the one who knocks, the door will be opened.

These words teach us about the character of God. He's the kind of God you can ask to help you through a tough situation. He's the kind of God who can be found when you need him. He's the kind of God who invites you to knock at his door. Jesus wants us to know that God loves us enough to allow even sinful, broken people like us to come before him with our needs and desires. It's okay to ask. God doesn't hide up in heaven. If you knock on his door, He will let you in.

That's not the kind of God many people in Jesus' day believed in, and from what I see in our culture, it's also not how some people understand God today. Some people think that God is inaccessible, far away and high above any earthly concerns, but Jesus called God Father and taught us how deeply He cares for us, who are his beloved children. Some people fear God and try to hide from his unquenchable wrath, but Jesus told us God blesses us each day and invites us to ask him for anything we need. Some people doubt God's existence or try to remake him into their own image, but Jesus gave us permission to knock at God's door, trusting that He will allow us to enter into an eternal, loving relationship with him.

I don't know what you are asking God for today, but I know that He is listening. I don't know how desperately you might be seeking after him right now, but I know He is drawing close to you. I don't know why you are knocking at his door, but I know He will open it joyfully and let you in. Jesus died and rose again to make this kind of relationship with God possible. So, don't be afraid to ask, seek and knock. God is waiting for you.

Father, You are glorious and holy, and You are loving and kind. Thank You for inviting me to know You and to come before You with all my needs. I am knocking at Your door, believing in my heart that You listen to me and love me. I pray in Jesus' name. Amen.

Matthew 7:9-12

Which of you, if your son asks for bread, will give him a stone? Or if he asks for a fish, will give him a snake? If you, then, though you are evil, know how to give good gifts to your children, how much more will your Father in heaven give good gifts to those who ask him! So in everything, do to others what you would have them do to you, for this sums up the Law and the Prophets.

The Year of our Lord 2020 was a hard one. From political divisions to global pandemic to racial injustice to protests and riots, plus sprinkle in a presidential election, hurricane season and a summer without baseball, this year has been one to remember and forget. Our nation endured hardship and anxiety in ways both deeply personal and widespread across every segment of society. No one is to blame for illness or the weather, but how we choose to respond to hardship and how we treat one another goes a long way toward determining the condition of our world. Which is why Jesus summed up God's moral wisdom in the Golden Rule.

If we would but treat people of another race the way we want them to treat us, most racial injustice would be eliminated. If we would speak of political adversaries the way we wish they would speak of us, there would be significantly less hostility in our culture. If we would tell the truth, plainly and simply, the way we would like others to, we could start believing more of what we hear.

At the same time, if we all listened to and obeyed Jesus, we would treat other people more like the way God treats us, with generosity, kindness and mercy. We would give good gifts to our children and to people in need. We would ask for help when we need it and trust that people would be kind to us. Jesus gave us a glimpse into how it could be, how it should be in our broken world, and that glimpse of a better humanity is really a reflection of God, the Giver of good gifts. May we follow Jesus as best and as often as we can, and pray that others will join us in faith and righteousness.

Thank You, Jesus, for speaking wisdom into my heart. Teach me to treat others with love and kindness just as I pray they will act toward me. Heal Your world and bring us peace, through Your mighty name. Amen.

Matthew 7:13-14

Enter through the narrow gate. For wide is the gate and broad is the road that leads to destruction, and many enter through it. But small is the gate and narrow the road that leads to life, and only a few find it.

Following the crowd is usually pretty easy. The wide gate and broad road is crowded with lots of people who will cheer you on if you go with the flow of culture and fit in with the latest ideas. It's Easy Street, and when you go there, no one will criticize you or push you aside or call you foolish. That is, so long as you follow the ways of the world and stay on the broad road with everyone else.

Following Jesus, on the other hand, takes courage, perseverance and faith. He told us it won't be easy. Jesus is the small gate through which we must enter, and God's word is the narrow road that leads to life. The way of life is narrow not because Jesus wants to keep people out, but because going that way requires faith and devotion. It means ignoring the crowd, leaving the wide way of the world and choosing instead the often difficult way of God. Following Jesus calls for submission and obedience. It requires denying yourself and taking up your cross. Walking down the narrow road means accepting God's will for your life, instead of insisting on your own desires.

You will have lots of opportunities to decide which road to take. The temptation to follow the crowd down Easy Street will always be there. You might even have friends or family members who think you are foolish to keep carrying your cross down the narrow way of following Jesus. Truth is, you may have taken an occasional detour down the broad road. We all have. But if you turn back to Jesus and the wisdom of God's word, you will find the way of life again. It can be hard to stay on that path, but Jesus promises you that it leads to a better life and to an everlasting life.

Father, help me to stay focused on You and the way forward that You know is best. Forgive me for going astray and wanting an easier way through life. Give me strength and courage to follow Jesus, especially when it feels like I am the only one. I ask this in His good name. Amen.

Matthew 7:15-20

Watch out for false prophets. They come to you in sheep's clothing, but inwardly they are ferocious wolves. By their fruit you will recognize them. Do people pick grapes from thornbushes, or figs from thistles? Likewise, every good tree bears good fruit, but a bad tree bears bad fruit. A good tree cannot bear bad fruit, and a bad tree cannot bear good fruit. Every tree that does not bear good fruit is cut down and thrown into the fire. Thus, by their fruit you will recognize them.

Hard times bring out the best and the worst in people. In the same way, the true condition of a person's heart becomes more visible during times of crisis. As our nation stumbled through the pandemic and faced the fires of racial injustice, people were forced to take a stand and to put their words into action in ways that reveal what lives inside their hearts. Some of what emerged was beautiful and inspiring. Some was ugly and sad.

Jesus is never fooled by pretense. He sees right through hypocrisy. Jesus knows what is in people's hearts and can immediately tell the difference between good fruit and bad. We like this about Jesus, because it means that bad people with insincere hearts won't get away with their deceptions and grandstanding. Then again, neither will we.

In another place, Jesus said his followers are like branches growing out of him, who is the true vine (John 15:1-8). So long as we stay connected to him, we will be fruitful, but if we wander away and become disconnected from the Vine, we won't be able to produce anything good. That's how it is with good trees, too. If you keep yourself rooted in the rich soil of God's word, drink deeply of the Spirit's living water and let God's glory shine down on you, then you will remain healthy and will be able to do good things that please God and to show genuine love to others. Being a good tree doesn't come naturally for us, but staying connected to Jesus through prayer, worship and spiritual devotion keeps us rooted and healthy. That's the only way to live a truly good life with a good heart that produces good fruit.

Father, You are good all the time. Help me to stay connected to Jesus and to do what is good in Your sight. Teach me to love others and to make Your world better through my actions and my words. I pray this in Jesus' name and for His glory. Amen.

Matthew 7:21-23

Not everyone who says to me, "Lord, Lord," will enter the kingdom of heaven, but only the one who does the will of my Father who is in heaven. Many will say to me on that day, "Lord, Lord, did we not prophesy in your name and in your name drive out demons and in your name perform many miracles?" Then I will tell them plainly, "I never knew you. Away from me, you evildoers!"

Some people love to be associated with the latest trend, whether it's a popular cause or a political movement or eating gluten-free or saving the rainforests. They say the right catch-phrases, wear t-shirts emblazoned with the popular viewpoint, and post on social media about how dedicated they are to the movement of the moment. But when trends change, so do they. Then it's on to the next fad they hope will make them cool or socially relevant. In the end, they might not really care about any of the causes they profess to support, but they sure do care about what other people think about them.

That seems to be the kind of insincere faith and religious showboating that bothered Jesus. There are people who want the benefits and blessings that Jesus promised but don't have hearts deeply committed to him. They want to be associated with the King of Kings but don't really have faith and aren't willing to live a life of obedience, sacrifice and service. As He neared the end of his long sermon, Jesus wanted to be sure his audience understood what they were signing up for. If you want to follow Jesus, it takes more than calling him "Lord." It means having a transformed heart. It means trusting God each day. It means submitting yourself to God's will. It means loving others, even those who don't like you. It means choosing the narrow road of faith and righteousness.

Those of us with sincere, devoted faith can still fall into this trap of paying Jesus lip service and not truly serving God's will. Sometimes we go through the motions of faith and worship, but our hearts aren't really in it. That's when we need to re-read Jesus' words and remind ourselves what it means to call him Lord. He came to rule over every part of your life, purchasing you from sin and death as your Savior and calling you to follow him as your only Lord and Master. That takes commitment, and it leads to eternal blessing.

Jesus, You are my Lord and my Savior. Without You, I would be lost and hopeless. Thank You for giving me new life and showing me how to follow God's will. I give all I am and all I have in service to Your name. Amen.

Matthew 7:24-29

Therefore everyone who hears these words of mine and puts them into practice is like a wise man who built his house on the rock. The rain came down, the streams rose, and the winds blew and beat against that house; yet it did not fall, because it had its foundation on the rock. But everyone who hears these words of mine and does not put them into practice is like a foolish man who built his house on sand. The rain came down, the streams rose, and the winds blew and beat against that house, and it fell with a great crash.

When Jesus had finished saying these things, the crowds were amazed at his teaching, because he taught as one who had authority, and not as their teachers of the law.

This little parable speaks for itself without much interpretation or complicated application from a preacher like me. Are you going to live like the wise person who puts Jesus' words into practice? Will you build your life on the firm foundation of obedience? Choosing to follow Jesus should be simple, but obedience to God's word requires a steadfast determination, every single day, to set aside what we may desire or what the world may suggest and actually follow Jesus' teaching. Look back through all the hard and surprising things Jesus just finished saying in the Sermon on the Mount and consider how you can put them into practice. Don't just agree that they are nice ideas. Don't just hope that others will follow Jesus' teaching. Live his words out today in your life.

There is one aspect of Jesus' parable that is worth highlighting so we don't miss it: both houses, the wise man's and the foolish man's, were hit by the storm. You can picture them built almost side-by-side on the same river bank. One has a strong foundation, dug deep down to rest on bedrock. The other has no foundation, just sitting on the loose sand. Then the rain falls and the wind blows and the river floods, and both houses are put to the test.

We have learned, maybe in ways we never before imagined, that every life gets tested by storms. We all endure hardship and suffering and loss. If your life has a strong foundation of faith in Jesus, resting on the bedrock of obedience to God's word, then you will have strength to weather the storm without fear or anxiety.

Father, You are my strong foundation. Help me to listen to Jesus and to follow His example in all I do today. Give me strength and a willing spirit to do what You know is good. I ask this through my Lord Jesus Christ. Amen.

THE PARABLES OF JESUS

Jesus loved to tell stories. We know them as parables, stories that teach God's truth. Some of his parables have become part of popular culture, like the prodigal son and the good Samaritan. Jesus' parables are true stories, even though the stories themselves are not true. That is, the stories Jesus told didn't actually happen. Instead, his parables point us to truth. Truth about God. Truth about ourselves. Truth about life in the Kingdom. Jesus told parables because people like stories and because they are easy to remember. He also told stories because some truths are easier to accept when we see them acted out in someone's life. May Jesus' parables speak truth into your heart.

Matthew 13:1-9

That same day Jesus went out of the house and sat by the lake. Such large crowds gathered around him that he got into a boat and sat in it, while all the people stood on the shore. Then he told them many things in parables, saying: "A farmer went out to sow his seed. As he was scattering the seed, some fell along the path, and the birds came and ate it up. Some fell on rocky places, where it did not have much soil. It sprang up quickly, because the soil was shallow. But when the sun came up, the plants were scorched, and they withered because they had no root. Other seed fell among thorns, which grew up and choked the plants. Still other seed fell on good soil, where it produced a crop—a hundred, sixty or thirty times what was sown. Whoever has ears, let them hear."

Most of us aren't farmers who sow seeds in our fields, but we are people who cast about words everywhere we go. We make small talk with strangers. We share intimate conversations with loved ones. We say kind things to people in church. We say unkind things to people we have trouble loving. We utter countless words day after day, giving little thought to where our little seeds fall and what sort of fruit they might produce.

Jesus was deliberate with His words. He spoke only true words that would lead people closer to God. This parable, the first recorded in the Gospels, is actually a parable about parables, a story about how Jesus used words. And He wasn't talking about any old words; He wanted us to think about the life-giving power of his word. That is, the word of God, the Good News, the Gospel. Jesus was like the farmer spreading the seed of truth, some of which fell on good, healthy soil and some that fell on hard-packed, rocky or thorny ground. Wherever Jesus went, whomever He spoke with, He always spoke true, life-giving words.

And we are like that farmer too, spreading seeds all around. Hopefully, the words we speak are true and life-giving.

Seeds of good news, hope, peace and love. You can't control how other people hear your words or the condition of the soil in their hearts, but you are responsible for the words you speak. May your good words take root and produce fruit.

Thank You, Jesus, for speaking good words of truth and salvation. I pray that Your word would take root in my life so I can grow good fruit. Help me to share Your words with others and to speak with love. I pray this for Your glory and in Your name. Amen.

Matthew 13:10-12

The disciples came to him and asked, "Why do you speak to the people in parables?"

He replied, "Because the knowledge of the secrets of the kingdom of heaven has been given to you, but not to them. Whoever has will be given more, and they will have an abundance. Whoever does not have, even what they have will be taken from them."

I'm not a big fan of modern art. A few squiggly lines on an empty canvas doesn't mean a whole lot to me. Nor do I appreciate a nonsensical sculpture that's meant to evoke some abstract feeling. Maybe I'm not trying hard enough, but I prefer art that I can understand and that looks beautiful. Jesus told parables to communicate difficult and sometimes controversial theological truths. His stories are easy to follow, with simple plots and familiar characters, but the spiritual truth behind them may seem obscure or hidden. In that way, Jesus' parables share a bit in common with abstract art.

But Jesus didn't tell parables to confuse people. He wasn't trying to be cute or deceptive or mysterious. In fact, just the opposition. Jesus told stories so people could understand spiritual realities that would otherwise be hard to put into words. Sometimes, our hearts can grasp what our minds can't comprehend. But you do have work at it. You do have to listen to the story and empathize with the characters and imagine what it would be like to experience what happens to them. Jesus didn't tell parables to keep the "secrets of the kingdom of heaven" hidden, but to reveal those wonderful, life-giving secrets to those who, by faith, can hear and understand.

In the same way, we don't study the Bible so that after years of academic discipline we might achieve a complete, scientifically-precise knowledge of God. No, we read the Bible to hear God's voice speaking into our hearts. As the Psalmist put it, "Deep calls to deep in the roar of your waterfalls" (Psalm

42:7). Scripture, especially Jesus' parables, reaches into our souls and draws us closer to God's unfathomable glory and grace.

Father, I will never reach the end of Your majesty and perfect love. Thank You for revealing Yourself to me through Your word and through Jesus my Savior. Help me to seek after You with all my heart and to rejoice in the beauty of Your word. Through Jesus I pray. Amen.

Matthew 13:13-17

This is why I speak to them in parables:
Though seeing, they do not see;
 though hearing, they do not hear or understand.
In them is fulfilled the prophecy of Isaiah:
'You will be ever hearing but never understanding;
 you will be ever seeing but never perceiving.
For this people's heart has become calloused;
 they hardly hear with their ears,
 and they have closed their eyes.
Otherwise they might see with their eyes,
 hear with their ears,
 understand with their hearts
and turn, and I would heal them.'
 But blessed are your eyes because they see, and your ears because they hear. For truly I tell you, many prophets and righteous people longed to see what you see but did not see it, and to hear what you hear but did not hear it.

I think Jesus often felt like the old cowboy who led his thirsty horse to water but then couldn't make her drink. In a lot of ways, that's the story of Old Testament prophecy too. Over and over, God showed his people the right way to live and called them to trust in his power and mercy, only to have them ignore his words and go their own way. Then, Jesus came offering salvation and telling stories about the grace of God, but many people heard without understanding and saw without perceiving. If they would only turn to me, God said, I would heal them.

The other side of this coin is that those who do understand, who do see and hear and believe Jesus, get to taste what even the most faithful prophets of the Old Testament never could. We get to experience the glory and grace of God, through friendship with Jesus Christ, in the power of the Holy

Spirit. What a wonderful blessing to have eyes that see and ears that hear the Good News.

For those who haven't yet tasted the goodness of God, there is still hope. God's mercy is not a limited time offer, at least not in this life. People who don't yet know Jesus as their Savior are still being invited to "see with their eyes, hear with their ears, understand with their hearts and turn" to God in faith. God is still waiting for them with open arms, ready to heal and save.

Gracious Lord, I have hope and joy in my heart because of the mercy You show me through Jesus. Thank You for saving me and blessing me. Help me to show others the way to Jesus, so they can turn to You, through Jesus the Savior. Amen.

Matthew 13:24-26

Jesus told them another parable: "The kingdom of heaven is like a man who sowed good seed in his field. But while everyone was sleeping, his enemy came and sowed weeds among the wheat, and went away. When the wheat sprouted and formed heads, then the weeds also appeared." ...

There are lots of reasons I wouldn't be a good farmer. Not enough patience. Too much dirt and manure. But especially the weeds. I can't stand finding weeds in my lawn, so I can't imagine watching a whole field full of valuable wheat infested by good-for-nothing weeds. I couldn't sleep until I had sprayed or chopped or pulled every last invader. Jesus understood. That's why the opening to this parable draws us in. We can picture the farmer fuming over his infested field. And just wait until he gets his hands on the enemy who sowed those weeds!

We also know right away what this story is really about. God created a good world where the people He loves can grow, flourish and love him, but the Enemy has sent a virus of evil and sin to infect God's world. Now, we have to live among the weeds. We strive to honor God and to do what is right, but so often our good intentions and faithful desires get choked out by temptation, hurt and sin. And while we would like to blame the Enemy and the bad people around us for all our problems, we have to admit that sometimes we act pretty weedy too.

The second half of the parable will help us understand Jesus' ultimate solution for evil in the world, but for now, we should be grateful to know that God planted us in his world on purpose and expects us to grow good fruit. The weeds may bother us and try our patience, but we can't use them as an excuse for not growing or not serving God's purposes. We are his wheat, planted in a good field to produce a crop to the glory of God. Weeds and all, we need to be who God created us to be.

Father in Heaven, You created me on purpose. Thank You for giving me what I need to serve You and to make Your world a better place. Give me strength to endure hardship and to resist temptation. In Jesus' name I pray. Amen.

Matthew 13:27-30

The owner's servants came to him and said, 'Sir, didn't you sow good seed in your field? Where then did the weeds come from?'
'An enemy did this,' he replied.
The servants asked him, 'Do you want us to go and pull them up?'
'No,' he answered, 'because while you are pulling the weeds, you may uproot the wheat with them. Let both grow together until the harvest. At that time I will tell the harvesters: First collect the weeds and tie them in bundles to be burned; then gather the wheat and bring it into my barn.'

This little story is one of Jesus' most profound and expansive parables. In just a few sentences, it deals with cosmology, theodicy and eschatology. Cosmology examines the beginning of time and the creation of the world. Jesus tells us that God created a good world where people can thrive and be fruitful in service to our Creator. Theodicy studies God's response to suffering and evil. Why does God let bad things happen in his good world? Why doesn't God just pull up all the weeds? Eschatology imagines the end of time and the final fulfillment of God's plan for this world. Jesus tells us in the parable that there will be a divine judgment in which the weeds will be destroyed and the good wheat will be harvested into God's glorious presence. That's a lot of ground to cover in one parable.

If we are honest, we may not really like what Jesus is telling us here. Most people tend to side with the servant who wants to go pull up all the weeds. Why let evil persist? Why allow bad things to happen to good people? Why doesn't God do something about all the suffering and hurt in his world? Why does God put up with racism, domestic violence, sexual assault, abortion, greed and corruption? There are just so many weeds!

Jesus assures us of two things in this parable. First, the weeds are here to stay, for now. We don't have to like them, but we do have to put up with them and learn to live good lives despite the bad happening around us. Second, God has a perfect plan to deal with evil. Judgment will fall on this world, and God will rightly divide the wheat from the weeds. That isn't our job, and we can't control when it will happen, but we can know for sure that one day Jesus will return to take his followers to heaven where there will be no more weeds.

Good Father, thank You for creating this world where I can know You and love You. Give me strength to endure the hardships and hurts of this life, and give me hope for eternity. I trust in Your goodness and grace, through Jesus my Savior. Amen.

Matthew 13:31-33

He told them another parable: "The kingdom of heaven is like a mustard seed, which a man took and planted in his field. Though it is the smallest of all seeds, yet when it grows, it is the largest of garden plants and becomes a tree, so that the birds come and perch in its branches."

He told them still another parable: "The kingdom of heaven is like yeast that a woman took and mixed into about sixty pounds of flour until it worked all through the dough."

Do you remember the young man who stood in front of the column of tanks sent by the Chinese government to break up the pro-democracy protest in Tiananmen Square? It was 1989, and Communism was collapsing around the world. In Beijing, however, the military was ordered to quiet the voices calling for freedom by any means necessary. That's when an unidentified young man, dressed in a white t-shirt, bravely stared down the tanks. His actions didn't liberate the Chinese people from tyranny, nor did they prevent the military from clearing the square of protesters, but those few moments of courage, as one man stood up for freedom, gave hope to the watching world. Sometimes, small things can be powerful.

Jesus spoke often about the kingdom of heaven, the active reign of God in the lives of his followers. When we obey God and follow Jesus, we are living in the kingdom of heaven. When we take up our cross and love our neighbors and lay down our lives for our friends, we are living in the kingdom of heaven. In some ways, the kingdom feels like a vast realm of glory and power, with Almighty God seated on his majestic throne. Far too often, however, it seems like the darkness of this world swallows up every glimmer of God's goodness. It may feel like our little acts of obedience to God just get swept away by the torrent of evil and sin.

Jesus knew otherwise. He knew that each little righteous deed and every loving word, each moment of courage and faithfulness, each spark of goodness in the kingdom of heaven, makes a difference. A little seed can grow into a huge tree. A pinch of yeast can work through the whole batch of dough. When you love your neighbor, each time you forgive, every word of encouragement, all your faithful prayers, any kindness you show to someone in need, every little act of Christ-like, God-honoring, Spirit-inspired goodness cuts through the darkness and expands the kingdom of heaven.

Thank You, God, for noticing each of the little ways I attempt to serve You and to love those around me. Help me to obey Your word and to follow the ways of Jesus, so I can help make Your world a little better each day. I pray this in Jesus' name. Amen.

Matthew 13:44-46

"The kingdom of heaven is like treasure hidden in a field. When a man found it, he hid it again, and then in his joy went and sold all he had and bought that field.

"Again, the kingdom of heaven is like a merchant looking for fine pearls. When he found one of great value, he went away and sold everything he had and bought it."

Our hearts are like our stomachs; they don't understand finances. When we want something, our hearts don't care how much it costs. In the same way, when we're hungry, we can be just as content with a $1 hotdog as with expensive prime rib in a fancy restaurant. Things in this world are worth whatever people will pay for them. A few dollars' worth of oil paints can become "priceless" when applied to canvas by a true master. Did you know the Mona Lisa is insured for nearly $1 billion? Is anything in this world worth that much? I guess it depends on whether you are listening to your heart or to your accountant!

Jesus told us that the kingdom of heaven is more valuable than buried treasure. Knowing God and being loved by him are priceless. The hope of eternity in God's glorious presence is worth more than fine pearls, gold and diamonds. None of this world's treasures can compare to God's perfect, unending love. The amazing truth about the kingdom of heaven is that Jesus paid the price for us to enter. We don't have to break the bank or sell our property or work all our lives to pay for a ticket. Jesus gives it to us for free.

These two little parables aren't about putting a monetary value on the kingdom of heaven, but Jesus is telling us how much knowing God is worth. Nothing in this world can compare. When our hearts behold the glory and grace of God through Jesus Christ, we desire just a taste of heaven more than all this world's luxury. Faith fills our hearts, and we come to understand the priceless worth of knowing God.

Thank You, Lord, for allowing me to know You and to taste Your goodness. I love You more than anything this world can offer. Protect me from the temptation of material things, and fill my heart with the hope of seeing You face-to-face in heaven. I pray in my Savior's name. Amen.

Matthew 13:47-50

"Once again, the kingdom of heaven is like a net that was let down into the lake and caught all kinds of fish. When it was full, the fishermen pulled it up on the shore. Then they sat down and collected the good fish in baskets, but threw the bad away. This is how it will be at the end of the age. The angels will come and separate the wicked from the righteous and throw them into the blazing furnace, where there will be weeping and gnashing of teeth."

Jesus talked far more about judgment, gnashing of teeth, blazing furnaces and hell than most of us are comfortable with. The whole concept of a final judgment upsets our modern, enlightened, tolerant sensibilities. There are no bad fish, just fish who do bad things! We might rather ignore some of what Jesus said than face the hard realities He so often taught, and when it comes to people being thrown into a blazing furnace, it might be easier for us just to look the other way. But Jesus said it, and we believe his words are true, so we better deal with it.

Anytime we read about the coming judgment of all mankind in the Bible, we should bear in mind two critical truths. First, you and I and everyone we know deserves every harsh judgment Jesus ever talked about. We are low-down, no-good sinners, and in God's perfect justice, He must condemn people like us to the blazing furnace. Eternal suffering and separation from God is our rightful due. Second, Jesus died and rose again to save us from the fires of hell. If you have accepted Jesus' free offer of new life through faith in his name, then you don't need to fear the final judgment. Your sin has already been forgiven. You have already been redeemed. You have been declared righteous in God's sight. Not because you are good, but because Jesus paid the price to set you free, according to the wonderful grace of God.

Jesus came proclaiming good news, not judgment and

condemnation. Yes, there will be a final judgment, and some sinners will be forever cast away from God's glorious presence. That Biblical truth is undeniable, but so is the amazing assurance that Jesus came to save sinners. He came to make it possible for everyone who trusts in him to become good fish destined for everlasting peace in heaven. That's the good news Jesus taught and the message of salvation we still share today.

Father in Heaven, Your justice is perfect, and Your grace is wonderful. Thank You for forgiving my sin and promising me a place in heaven. Help me to share with others the good news of Jesus my Savior, through whom I pray. Amen.

Matthew 13:51-52

"Have you understood all these things?" Jesus asked.
"Yes," they replied.
He said to them, "Therefore every teacher of the law who has become a disciple in the kingdom of heaven is like the owner of a house who brings out of his storeroom new treasures as well as old."

Most people these days don't have treasure. I don't know anyone who has a chest full of jewels and gold coins. We might display a few cherished items in our homes, like antiques from a grandparent or souvenirs from a favorite vacation. Some people may keep expensive jewelry, fine china or collectible items that they consider valuable. I suppose those are types of treasure. From what I know of the culture Jesus lived in, very few of the people who listened to him had treasure either, not the kind you lock away in a storeroom or hide in a secret vault. Then again, Jesus never cared much for gold and silver. He didn't consider the things of this world as valuable as the true, lasting treasure of heaven.

For Jesus, God's word is a treasure worth seeking after and holding onto. The teachers of the law, those who spent their time studying and educating others about scripture, held vast wealth in the storerooms of their hearts and minds. They knew God's word inside and out, from beginning to end. Their Bible, what we call the Old Testament, revealed God's character and pointed ahead to the coming of the Messiah. How wonderful it would be, then, if a teacher of the law recognized Jesus as the promised Messiah and could add to their treasure chest the good news of the kingdom of heaven. Their storeroom would be overflowing with the priceless treasure of God's word.

We have both old and new treasure, and we shouldn't take it for granted. God's word, the Old and New Testaments, help us know God. Even more precious, scripture helps us enter into an eternal loving relationship with God through Jesus Christ. As we read the Bible, we hear God speaking to us, and we discover His will for our lives. We find promises that give us hope through suffering and strength when burdens weigh us down. What's amazing about the treasure of scripture is that it becomes even more valuable when we share it with others. Then God's word has the power to change hearts and to offer sinners grace.

Father in Heaven, thank You for revealing Yourself to me in Your word and for speaking truth into my heart. Draw me back to the Bible often, and show me opportunities to share the life-giving treasure of Your word with others. I ask this through Jesus my Lord. Amen.

Matthew 18:12-14

"What do you think? If a man owns a hundred sheep, and one of them wanders away, will he not leave the ninety-nine on the hills and go to look for the one that wandered off? And if he finds it, truly I tell you, he is happier about that one sheep than about the ninety-nine that did not wander off. In the same way your Father in heaven is not willing that any of these little ones should perish."

How do we square this Jesus with the one who talks about burning weeds in a blazing furnace? Why would a God of judgment and wrath send a Shepherd to search for one lost sheep? Truth is, we love this Jesus, the Good Shepherd who leaves the 99 to "seek and save the lost" (Luke 19:10). We would rather ignore the Jesus who talks about the fires of hell and the gnashing of teeth. We prefer the God of grace to the God of judgment, but Jesus doesn't let us pick and choose which aspects of God's perfect, unchanging nature we want to hear about. Jesus told the whole truth about God, and that means we need to hear about God's perfect justice that leads him to judge sinners for their sin, rightly condemning those who never repent or seek forgiveness. Without God's justice, He could not be good, and we wouldn't understand the difference between right and wrong. At the same time, God's heart is loving and kind, full of mercy for sinners, "not willing that any of these little ones should perish."

That's why Jesus came into the world. He came to be the Good Shepherd who looks for the lost sheep. Jesus is happy every time a sinner is saved, because God takes no delight in judgment but delights to show us grace. God's heart overflows with love for you and me and all the other sinners in this world. The Good Shepherd came to save us.

This little parable teaches us about God's heart and about Jesus' mission. It also reminds us that Jesus invites his followers to join the search and rescue operation. Now, the church works alongside the Good Shepherd, caring for his sheep and searching for those who wander off. When one is found, when Jesus saves a sinner, we join in the heavenly rejoicing.

Lord Jesus, I praise You for Your mercy and grace. Thank You for finding me when I was lost and washing away my sin. Show me how I can help You search for other lost sheep and bring them home to Your loving arms. I pray in Your good name. Amen.

Matthew 18:21-27

Then Peter came to Jesus and asked, "Lord, how many times shall I forgive my brother or sister who sins against me? Up to seven times?"
Jesus answered, "I tell you, not seven times, but seventy-seven times.
"Therefore, the kingdom of heaven is like a king who wanted to settle accounts with his servants. As he began the settlement, a man who owed him ten thousand bags of gold was brought to him. Since he was not able to pay, the master ordered that he and his wife and his children and all that he had be sold to repay the debt.
"At this the servant fell on his knees before him. 'Be patient with me,' he begged, 'and I will pay back everything.' The servant's master took pity on him, canceled the debt and let him go." ...

It's hard to imagine how anyone could accrue a debt of 10,000 bags of gold. Just so we understand the enormous burden of the debt Jesus described, let me share a few Biblical calculations. The actual word used here is "talent," which was the largest unit of weight measurement in Jesus' day. Scholars believe a talent was roughly equivalent to 50 pounds, so 10,000 talents would be 250 tons of gold. Gold has recently been valued at a record high of more than $1,900 per ounce. So, in modern financial terms, the servant owed the king roughly $15.2 billion! Ouch. Jesus used such an outrageous sum to catch the attention of his listeners, but also to make a theological point that we may struggle to grasp or that we may choose to ignore. Jesus was comparing the servant's financial debt to the spiritual debt we owe God because of our sin.

The servant's debt teaches us two things. First, sin is really, really bad. The Holy God who created us can't just overlook our sin or wish it away, because sin covers us with a filthy grime so sticky and vile that God, who loves us, could never allow us to be near him. Our only hope is to be washed clean, but we don't have enough soap. In financial terms, we could never pay off what we owe. Second, God's grace to forgive our sin is truly amazing. He didn't just write-off our sin like some accounting trick to erase the debt. Our spiritual debt still had to be paid, so Jesus paid that enormous, unfathomable debt on our behalf.

Jesus told this parable in response to Peter's question about how often we need to forgive someone who wrongs us. Peter thought he was being generous by suggesting seven times. It's hard to forgive, to cancel a debt someone owes us. Seven times sounds pretty magnanimous until we realize just how much grace God has shown us.

Gracious Father, in my sinfulness, I owe You more than I can imagine or could ever repay. But what joy I have knowing that You canceled my debt because Jesus died for me. Thank You for Your grace and love. Teach me to forgive others, in Jesus' name. Amen.

Matthew 18:28-35

"But when that servant went out, he found one of his fellow servants who owed him a hundred silver coins. He grabbed him and began to choke him. 'Pay back what you owe me!' he demanded.

"His fellow servant fell to his knees and begged him, 'Be patient with me, and I will pay it back.'

"But he refused. Instead, he went off and had the man thrown into prison until he could pay the debt. When the other servants saw what had happened, they were outraged and went and told their master everything that had happened.

"Then the master called the servant in. 'You wicked servant,' he said, 'I canceled all that debt of yours because you begged me to. Shouldn't you have had mercy on your fellow servant just as I had on you?' In anger his master handed him over to the jailers to be tortured, until he should pay back all he owed.

"This is how my heavenly Father will treat each of you unless you forgive your brother or sister from your heart."

Forgiving someone who has hurt you may be the hardest thing you ever have to do. Especially, if that person has hurt you over and over again. Remember, Jesus told this parable to answer Peter's question about how often we need to forgive someone. Our natural reaction to being hurt is to strike back or to run away. Those responses may spare us from being hurt again, but that's not what Jesus asks of us. He wants us to forgive others, just as God forgives us. (It's important to say, Jesus is not telling anyone to stay in an abusive relationship and continue to be hurt. You can forgive and also protect yourself from being hurt again.)

In Jesus' parable, financial debt stands for the hurt caused by someone else's sin. It might be easier for us to cancel a debt than to truly forgive someone from our hearts. We can't erase the memory of angry words or hateful actions. We can't forget what others have done to us or how they made us feel.

Forgiveness is like canceling a financial debt in the sense that once we have offered to forgive, we no longer have a right to hold the sin against that person. If you burn the promissory note, you can't write a new one for the same debt. Forgiveness may not feel like a legal or financial transaction, but somehow our hearts need to treat it that way.

The hardest line of this passage is the last one. Jesus tells us that God won't forgive us if we refuse to forgive others. This isn't a way to earn or lose salvation, but Jesus wants us to take to heart just how important forgiveness is. In fact, it's so important to God that He sent his own Son to die on the cross so He could forgive our enormous spiritual debt. If for no other reason, we should forgive others out of gratitude for God's grace toward us and out of obedience to Jesus' words. It's never easy to forgive, but remember what it cost God to forgive you.

Thank You, Jesus, for paying the price for my sin. Teach me to forgive others, just as You show unending mercy to me. You are my Savior, and I love You. Amen.

Matthew 20:1-7

"For the kingdom of heaven is like a landowner who went out early in the morning to hire workers for his vineyard. He agreed to pay them a denarius for the day and sent them into his vineyard.

"About nine in the morning he went out and saw others standing in the marketplace doing nothing. He told them, 'You also go and work in my vineyard, and I will pay you whatever is right.' So they went.

"He went out again about noon and about three in the afternoon and did the same thing. About five in the afternoon he went out and found still others standing around. He asked them, 'Why have you been standing here all day long doing nothing?'

"'Because no one has hired us,' they answered.

"He said to them, 'You also go and work in my vineyard.'" …

    The life of a day-laborer must be rooted in faith. Imagine not knowing when you wake up in the morning where you will work or if you will be hired to work at all. Imagine worrying that if no one hires you that day, you won't have enough money to buy food for your family. When Jesus taught us to pray for "daily bread," He was thinking about people like the vineyard workers in this parable who don't know whether each new day will bring abundance or want. That sort of life must require a lot of faith.

    Most of us give little thought to where our next meal will come from. We may have a hard time relating to the concept of praying for daily bread or wondering each morning if we will be given a job. But we can relate to being a worker. We know what it's like to be rewarded for productive labor, whether it's in school or in a factory, out in a farm field or in a business office. Our culture values hard work and productivity, and we know that gainful employment is how we provide for our families. Jesus valued hard work too. Many of his parables, like this one, focus on the lives of workers, servants, farmers and merchants. God created us with the ability to be productive. He gives us strength to work. He blesses the labor of our hands. Jesus understood that it's good for people to work, whether to earn income, to care for your family or to complete your education.

As we read the rest of this parable, we will see that it teaches us about God's grace, but let's not overlook how God, represented in the story by the vineyard owner, calls us to lead productive lives. Some are still growing and learning. Some hold steady jobs. Some care for their families. Some own or manage businesses. Some have retired from careers and found news ways to be productive. Whatever work you do each day, remember that your labors fulfill, in large measure, God's calling and purpose for your life.

Father, help me to work hard and contribute to the good of Your world. Thank You for giving me skill, strength and motivation to labor for Your glory and for the good of the people I love. Bless my work, in Jesus' name. Amen.

Matthew 20:8-12

"When evening came, the owner of the vineyard said to his foreman, 'Call the workers and pay them their wages, beginning with the last ones hired and going on to the first.'

"The workers who were hired about five in the afternoon came and each received a denarius. So when those came who were hired first, they expected to receive more. But each one of them also received a denarius. When they received it, they began to grumble against the landowner. 'These who were hired last worked only one hour,' they said, 'and you have made them equal to us who have borne the burden of the work and the heat of the day.'" ...

Most people aren't paid what they're worth. Some get far too little. Others make way too much. On the relative scale of salary comparisons, there's precious little justice. Think about nurses caring for patients in the ICU: there's no way they are paid enough. What about the young Super Bowl champion quarterback who recently signed a $500 million contract... to play football? Then again, if you agree to work for a certain wage, you don't have a right to complain about what you are paid at the end of the day. The struggle comes when you start to compare what you make or what you have or what opportunities you are given against someone else. Life isn't fair, especially when it comes to money.

Jesus put his finger squarely on one of the most sensitive spots in the human heart. Call it the fairness nerve or the justice bone. Jesus knows how quickly we humans get bent out of shape the second someone else gets treated better than us. If I work twice as much as her, I better get paid twice as much! How dare you pay him as much as me! Even as we listen to Jesus' story, we can't help but side with the workers who bore "the burden of the work and the heat of the day." In a perfectly fair and just world, they are right to be upset, we think. Except that this world is not perfectly fair or just.

Jesus will answer our complaints in the last few lines of his parable, but for now, let's remember to be cautious with comparisons and to take a breath before crying about fairness. If we are honest, most of us end up on the good side of many unfair situations. We come out ahead at least as often as we get short-changed. Sure, there are exceptions, and you might have a right to complain about some of the hardships in your life, but if Jesus is your Savior, then you have already been blessed far more than you deserve.

Gracious Father, forgive me for wanting what others have and complaining about what I think I deserve. Your love is enough. Help me to be content with what I have and to be grateful for all the blessings You bring me, through Jesus my Savior. Amen.

Matthew 20:13-16

"But he answered one of them, 'I am not being unfair to you, friend. Didn't you agree to work for a denarius? Take your pay and go. I want to give the one who was hired last the same as I gave you. Don't I have the right to do what I want with my own money? Or are you envious because I am generous?'
"So the last will be first, and the first will be last."

We love the generosity of God. He blesses us with good things day after day. He chooses to love us despite our sinfulness. He allows us to catch glimpses of his glory and fills us with hope for an eternity in his wonderful presence. God treats us better than we deserve, and we love that about God. Generosity is a facet of God's amazing grace about which we joyfully sing. Except when God shows generosity to someone else. We don't sing quite so joyfully when God offers grace to someone we think doesn't deserve it. Why would God be kind to a mean person? Or to someone who lies, cheats and steals? It isn't fair that God would be generous to someone who doesn't work very hard or doesn't treat people nicely or doesn't pray as often as we do. We love the generosity of God, except when He shows it to someone else.

The workers in Jesus' parable weren't treated fairly by the vineyard owner. He paid them each the same wage, even though some had only worked part of the day. Maybe the vineyard owner has a right to do what he wants with his own money, but it's still not fair, especially to the workers who labored hard all day long. They worked more, so they should be paid more, right? Of course, Jesus' parable is not about economics or fair employment practices. He isn't trying to teach business owners how to treat their employees. No, Jesus is teaching us about God's grace. And God's grace isn't fair. In fact, that's exactly what makes it grace. God loves us more than we deserve. He generously gives good things to sinners like us, not because we have worked hard for it or because we are such good people who deserve to be blessed, but simply because He loves to love us.

Grace isn't fair, and as recipients of God's amazing grace, we have no right to demand that He withhold grace from someone else, someone who is just as undeserving of God's love as we are. Be grateful for how generous God has been to you. Rejoice in the grace you have received. And when God generously blesses someone else, rejoice that He has enough love to share with the whole world.

Father in heaven, You are generous and kind. You love me far more than I deserve. Help me to rejoice when You show love to others and to remember how much You love me, through Jesus my Savior. Amen.

Matthew 21:28-32

"What do you think? There was a man who had two sons. He went to the first and said, 'Son, go and work today in the vineyard.'

"'I will not,' he answered, but later he changed his mind and went.

"Then the father went to the other son and said the same thing. He answered, 'I will, sir,' but he did not go.

"Which of the two did what his father wanted?"

"The first," they answered.

Jesus said to them, "Truly I tell you, the tax collectors and the prostitutes are entering the kingdom of God ahead of you. For John came to you to show you the way of righteousness, and you did not believe him, but the tax collectors and the prostitutes did. And even after you saw this, you did not repent and believe him."

Have you ever lied on a survey? Well, of course, you haven't lied, but have you ever varnished the truth a bit to impress the person conducting the survey? Professional pollsters have various terms for this, including the "halo effect" where people answer questions to make themselves look better than they really are, and "social desirability bias" where people give dishonest answers to avoid sounding weird or politically incorrect. Maybe we wouldn't do that, but we might understand why other people might claim to be what they are not or say they will do something they never actually do. Unfulfilled good intentions and broken promises don't amount to much more than lies and deception.

For Jesus, obedience is a matter of action and follow-through. Just saying you are going to do something doesn't count. God is not impressed or fooled by empty promises. Actions, as the saying goes and as Jesus' parable confirms, speak louder than words. The second son told his father what he wanted to hear, maybe to save face or to avoid an argument. He said he would go work in the vineyard, but then he didn't do it. The second son not only disobeyed his father, but he also lied to his face. The first son initially refused to obey, but then he changed his mind and obeyed. That is, he repented.

Maybe you have been telling God for a long time that you will make a change in your life or break a bad habit or develop a new spiritual discipline. You might have good intentions and really want to follow through, but until you actually do it, until you finally put into practice what you have said you would do, your words don't count for anything. It's time to repent, to change your mind, by turning your words into actions and your good intentions into obedience. That's what Jesus is waiting for.

Thank You, Jesus, for being patient with me. I'm sorry that I don't always do what I say I will. Help me to learn true obedience by doing the things You ask me to do in Your word. I love You and want to bring honor to Your name. Amen.

Matthew 21:33-39

"Listen to another parable: There was a landowner who planted a vineyard. He put a wall around it, dug a winepress in it and built a watchtower. Then he rented the vineyard to some farmers and moved to another place. When the harvest time approached, he sent his servants to the tenants to collect his fruit.

"The tenants seized his servants; they beat one, killed another, and stoned a third. Then he sent other servants to them, more than the first time, and the tenants treated them the same way. Last of all, he sent his son to them. 'They will respect my son,' he said.

"But when the tenants saw the son, they said to each other, 'This is the heir. Come, let's kill him and take his inheritance.' So they took him and threw him out of the vineyard and killed him." ...

Possession, they say, is nine-tenth of the law. While that old saying probably wouldn't hold up in court, it does speak to a dark part of human nature that desires to have and to hold things that aren't rightfully ours and to exercise control over people and possessions simply because we can. That's not always a bad thing. For instance, it's good for church members to feel a sense of ownership over our shared ministries and church property. We know none of us actually, legally owns the church, but feeling that sort of responsibility motivates us to care for the building and to work hard at growing our ministries. On the other hand, a desire to own what is not ours (envy) can lead us into even more terrible sins, like theft and violence.

Jesus' parable builds on that sinful desire within each of us to expose a much larger problem in humanity. God created a good, beautiful world for us. He blesses us abundantly and gives us meaningful work that, along with his love for us, should fully satisfy our hearts. But we want more. We humans crave to possess and control and have our way with God's world. We earn money and believe it's ours. We buy things and hold them tightly in our fists. We even claim sovereignty over our own lives, as though we were not created in God's image to love and honor him. We act, even if we are too fearful to say it out loud, like God is dead and we are in charge.

As we read Jesus' parable, we can easily identify the tenants as the villains. How terrible they are! How greedy, ungrateful and violent. And yet, with every sin, we join their rebellion. Instead, we should follow the example of the landowner's servants, who willingly lay down their lives to obey their master. You belong to God, along with everything in this world. As Paul wrote, "You are not your own; you were bought at a price" (1 Corinthians 6:19-20). Stop listening to what your envious heart desires and embrace the good news that you belong to God through Jesus your Savior.

Almighty God, You own all things, including my life. I rejoice that You are a loving and generous Master. Forgive me for my rebellion, and help me to serve Your good purposes, in the name of Jesus. Amen.

Matthew 21:40-42

"Therefore, when the owner of the vineyard comes, what will he do to those tenants?"

"He will bring those wretches to a wretched end," they replied, "and he will rent the vineyard to other tenants, who will give him his share of the crop at harvest time."

Jesus said to them, "Have you never read in the Scriptures:

"'The stone the builders rejected
has become the cornerstone;
the Lord has done this,
and it is marvelous in our eyes'?"

It's often easier for us to see faults in others than in ourselves. In the same way, the chief priests and elders who listened to Jesus' parable quickly handed down a verdict and swift punishment against the wretched tenants in the story while failing to recognize that Jesus told the parable against them. In Jesus' story, the tenants mistreated the servants and then killed the vineyard owner's own son. Jesus asked what judgment should fall on those greedy, violent tenants, and his listeners rightly called for judgment against them.

What the religious leaders failed to understand was their own sinfulness. The parable was like a spiritual mirror held up to the hearts of those who opposed Jesus and who would soon call for his crucifixion. Jesus was the stone the builders rejected. Many people in that generation wanted a different messiah, a savior who would fit their political, economic and social agendas. Just as their ancestors ignored and persecuted God's prophets, they turned against God's own Son.

Despite the specific application of the parable to First Century religious leaders, Jesus' words still speak to us. First, we are warned not to fall into the trap of judging others while overlooking our own sins. Even good, church-going folks sometimes ignore what Jesus says or think we have a better plan than God. Second, we are reminded that God provided for our salvation in a marvelous and surprising way. Through faith, we understand that Jesus is the perfect cornerstone, but there are many people who still reject him, wishing for a different sort of savior. We don't take that bait. We don't fall for the temptation to reshape Jesus into a culturally-acceptable, politically-correct spiritual guru. We preach Christ crucified, a stumbling block to some and foolishness to others, but good news and new life to those who believe.

Thank You, Father, for giving us such a marvelous Savior and for inviting me to find new life in Him. Show me the ways I fall short of Your perfect will, and help me to reflect Jesus' goodness and light more perfectly into the lives of others. In His name I pray. Amen.

Matthew 25:1-6

> *"At that time the kingdom of heaven will be like ten virgins who took their lamps and went out to meet the bridegroom. Five of them were foolish and five were wise. The foolish ones took their lamps but did not take any oil with them. The wise ones, however, took oil in jars along with their lamps. The bridegroom was a long time in coming, and they all became drowsy and fell asleep.*
>
> *"At midnight the cry rang out: 'Here's the bridegroom! Come out to meet him!'"* …

No one is born with patience. We have to learn that virtue through long, trying experiences. Like sitting at the DMV to renew your driver's license. They hand you a little slip of paper with number 487 on it, and the digital counter informs you that they are currently serving number 362. Every few minutes another number clicks by, and it feels like everyone in the room is holding their breath, watching the clock in the land where time stands still. That's how you learn patience, and there are no shortcuts.

Jesus' told this parable to teach us about waiting for His return and to warn us that no one knows when that moment will come. He is the bridegroom who will come one day to take his followers home to heaven. The ten virgins are excited for the wedding to begin, but unlike weddings in our day that usually start right on time, they don't know when to expect the bridegroom to arrive and kick-off the festivities. They have to wait, with lamps burning so they can see who is coming and how to find their way to the party. The wise virgins are prepared to wait, with extra oil for their lamps.

We need fuel to keep our faith burning while we watch and wait for Jesus. That fuel comes from reading stories in God's word of long-suffering, faithful disciples who have gone before us. We also find fuel for our lamps in the encouraging words of fellow believers who, like us, are learning patience.

We wait for Jesus to return, like the virgins watching for the bridegroom, and along the way, we wait for the smaller victories of answered prayers, lifted burdens, healing and reconciliation. Keep your lamp burning with extra fuel on hand. We don't know how long we may have to wait, but we do know for sure that the Lord is on his way.

Father, teach me to wait on You and to trust in Your perfect timing. You know what is best for me and when to give it. Help me to stand firm in faith. Come, Lord Jesus. I am ready and waiting for You. Amen.

Matthew 25:7-10

"Then all the virgins woke up and trimmed their lamps. The foolish ones said to the wise, 'Give us some of your oil; our lamps are going out.'

"'No,' they replied, 'there may not be enough for both us and you. Instead, go to those who sell oil and buy some for yourselves.'

"But while they were on their way to buy the oil, the bridegroom arrived. The virgins who were ready went in with him to the wedding banquet. And the door was shut." ...

Many people find great comfort and encouragement from the fellowship of the church. We love feeling included and cared for. We are blessed by those who walk with us through hard moments and who celebrate when we celebrate. In the church, we get to share life with people who also share our faith, and that's a joyful blessing. And yet, each of us also needs to have our own faith and to develop our own relationship with God through Jesus Christ. It's not enough to know people who have faith or to sit in the same pew with people who love Jesus. You also need to make that spiritual commitment for yourself.

The foolish virgins didn't plan ahead, and when the bridegroom finally arrives, their lamps have gone out. They thought they could just borrow some oil from the others, only to be told that that plan isn't going to work. In the end, they pay the price for not being ready. Jesus is warning us, and people everywhere, that we can't borrow someone's faith or ride coattails into eternity. You are responsible for your own spiritual life, for your own devotional habits, for your own times of prayer and worship. We get to walk this journey of faith together with other believers, but each of us has to walk.

We have to keep our lamps burning, fueled by the oil of faith, and we should also encourage others to do the same. You can pray for your friends, you can show them love in a thousand ways, and you can share with them the good news of

Jesus, but your faith can't save them. They need to open their hearts to Jesus, just as you and I have. That's why sharing the gospel matters so much. God calls us to help people find new life through faith in Jesus, and to find that new life before it's too late.

Thank You, Lord, for leading me to new life through Jesus my Savior. Help me to grow each day in faith and use me to share Jesus' love and message with people in need, so they can find new life too. I ask this in Jesus' name. Amen.

Matthew 25:11-13

"Later the others also came. 'Lord, Lord,' they said, 'open the door for us!'
"But he replied, 'Truly I tell you, I don't know you.'
"Therefore keep watch, because you do not know the day or the hour."

The coach calls timeout with 3 seconds on the clock. His team is down by one point with the championship on the line. He draws up a play to get his best shooter a clean look at the basket. The ball is passed in, shuffled across to the open man who turns, jumps and releases the ball just as the buzzer sounds. The ball swishes through the net, a perfect shot to win the game. Except that, upon further review, the ball was still in his hands when time expired. He made the shot, but it was too late. Wave off the basket. Game over. The other team wins. In sports, when time runs out, the game ends, and there are no do-overs or second chances.

God doesn't play games with the eternal destiny of people He loves, but Jesus warns us that time will run out for people to accept his offer of new life. Jesus died and rose again to offer salvation to every person on earth. He gives away this priceless gift free of charge and sends out his church to invite people everywhere to accept it. Each person needs only to say yes and accept the gift of new life through faith in Jesus. There are no catches and no fine print, no gimmicks or strings attached. People just have to open their hearts to Jesus before time runs out, before the door is shut forever. Time runs out for each person in one of two ways, either when they die or when Jesus returns. We have to accept Jesus' offer of salvation in this life, because when we die or Jesus returns, it will be too late.

Jesus told this parable to light a fire of urgency in the hearts of his listeners. The foolish virgins who don't keep their lamps lit and miss the wedding are like a flashing warning signal to those who don't yet believe in Jesus: Don't wait! Now is the time to accept Jesus as Lord and Savior. The parable should also give urgency to the church's mission. Jesus calls his followers to go and make disciples, to invite others to find salvation in Jesus before it's too late. We don't know when that day or hour will come, so we keep watch for Jesus as we share his love and message with the world.

Lord Jesus, I am watching for Your return and will rejoice in that day. For now, give me strength to serve You and to share the good news of salvation. Help me to show people who You are and to love them in Your name. Amen.

Matthew 25:14-18

"Again, it will be like a man going on a journey, who called his servants and entrusted his wealth to them. To one he gave five bags of gold, to another two bags, and to another one bag, each according to his ability. Then he went on his journey. The man who had received five bags of gold went at once and put his money to work and gained five bags more. So also, the one with two bags of gold gained two more. But the man who had received one bag went off, dug a hole in the ground and hid his master's money." ...

Some people might disagree, but I don't think there has been a more naturally gifted athlete in the last 50 years than Bo Jackson. You remember, "Bo knows..." football and baseball and running and swimming and tennis and on and on. He was bigger, faster and stronger than everyone else on the field and may have played his way into the hall of fame in both football and baseball had he not broken his hip in a freak injury caused most likely by his own prodigious strength. Bo Jackson could do it all on the field. He was a five bags of gold kind of athlete, blessed with a heaping measure of God-given talent.

Most of us, if we're honest, are more like the servants who received two bags or one bag of gold. And that's okay. Jesus' story is not about celebrating those rare individuals born with extraordinary talents, whether in sports or academics or personal charisma. God created you the way you are, special and unique in your own special ways. God wanted someone like you, with just the right set of gifts and abilities to be part of your family, to know your friends, to worship in your church, and to live in your community. One bag of gold servants matter to God just as much as those rare five baggers.

The question Jesus' story raises is what are you going to do with the gifts God has given you? Will you work hard, using your God-given talents for his glory? Will you invest what God has entrusted to you to help build his kingdom? Or, like the third servant, will you dig a hole and hide in it? Some people don't serve God as fruitfully as they could because they don't think they have much to offer. Sadly, the church often acts like the world by lifting up the loudest, strongest and most successful people, leaving others to feel unworthy and unwanted. Don't fall for that deception. God needs you, and his kingdom can only flourish when each of us puts to good use the gifts He has given.

Father, thank You for creating me with the ability to love You and to serve You. Show me how I can use my talents for Your glory and help me to encourage others to serve You too, in the name of Jesus. Amen.

Matthew 25:19-23

"After a long time the master of those servants returned and settled accounts with them. The man who had received five bags of gold brought the other five. 'Master,' he said, 'you entrusted me with five bags of gold. See, I have gained five more.'

"His master replied, 'Well done, good and faithful servant! You have been faithful with a few things; I will put you in charge of many things. Come and share your master's happiness!'

"The man with two bags of gold also came. 'Master,' he said, 'you entrusted me with two bags of gold; see, I have gained two more.'

"His master replied, 'Well done, good and faithful servant! You have been faithful with a few things; I will put you in charge of many things. Come and share your master's happiness!'" ...

We love this part of the parable. When we get to heaven, we imagine Jesus will say to us, "Well done, good and faithful servant." That would be a fitting summary of a life well-lived, having served our Master well and being told that we did good work for his kingdom. I hope all people of faith want to please Jesus by how we live and how we use the gifts He has given us. We serve Jesus at church, in our families, in our careers and as we live day by day in our community. All we do can be given in service to our Master, and if we work hard and devote ourselves to those things Jesus says truly matter, we can be confident we will hear a heavenly "Well done!"

There are two other aspects of the Master's words that we should notice. First, both faithful servants hear the same words of commendation. The Master is equally pleased with the two good and faithful workers, even though one earned five bags of gold and the other made only two. The servant who received two bags was not expected to earn five more. They each take what they are given and put it to work to double the Master's investment, and so they are each blessed equally and invited to share their Master's happiness. Second, notice that there is more work still to be done. The Master will now entrust more resources and responsibilities to each faithful servant. This may tell us that we will have work to do in heaven (like worship), but it may also indicate that Jesus' parable is just as much about tasks we accomplish in this life. As we show ourselves faithful, the Spirit entrusts us with greater kingdom responsibilities.

God has made an investment in you. He has given you gifts and abilities, and He has called you to honor him by loving your family, serving at church, doing good in the community, and being salt and light in every arena of your life. Good work that you accomplish for your Master's glory builds the kingdom. Then again, work left undone or poorly attempted wastes God's investment. However many bags of gold God has entrusted to you, may you be good and faithful in service to your Master.

Father in Heaven, thank You for trusting me to help build Your kingdom. Give me strength to work hard for Your glory and in the name of Jesus. Amen.

Matthew 25:24-30

"Then the man who had received one bag of gold came. 'Master,' he said, 'I knew that you are a hard man, harvesting where you have not sown and gathering where you have not scattered seed. So I was afraid and went out and hid your gold in the ground. See, here is what belongs to you.'

"His master replied, 'You wicked, lazy servant! So you knew that I harvest where I have not sown and gather where I have not scattered seed? Well then, you should have put my money on deposit with the bankers, so that when I returned I would have received it back with interest.

"'So take the bag of gold from him and give it to the one who has ten bags. For whoever has will be given more, and they will have an abundance. Whoever does not have, even what they have will be taken from them. And throw that worthless servant outside, into the darkness, where there will be weeping and gnashing of teeth.'"

We can fall short of God's expectations in different ways. Most often, we think of sin as doing something we shouldn't, but failing to do something we should can also be sinful. There are sins of commission (bad things we do) and sins of omission (good things we don't do). For instance, Jesus asks us to love our neighbors. That means to actively seek out ways to be kind and helpful to those in need. It's not enough simply to refrain from being mean to your neighbors. If you know someone could use a hand and you ignore them, you have failed to show love. In the same way, if you feel in your heart that God is leading you to reconcile a broken relationship or to speak truth into a hard situation or to do anything else out of obedience to God's leading, but you don't follow through, then you have fallen into the same trap as the lazy servant.

We often apply this parable to the whole of our lives, imagining God judging us based on how fruitful we have been throughout our lives with the resources He invested in us. That's a good and right interpretation, but we can also narrow the focus to any particular act of service God may set before us. The good, faithful servants do the Master's will, honoring him with obedience and hard work. The lazy servant, however, is given an opportunity to serve and chooses instead to do nothing. In burying the Master's bag of gold, the servant commits a sin of omission, failing to do anything worthwhile on behalf of the Master.

What is God asking you to do? What opportunities has He put before you to show love or to speak truth or to serve someone in need? Sometimes, we ignore these opportunities, burying them in the ground out of fear or laziness. God has placed the Holy Spirit in you to give you strength and wisdom to serve him. He has given you abilities and resources with which you can love others and help build the kingdom. As you prove yourself to be a good and faithful servant, God will trust you with greater kingdom work and invite you to share in his happiness.

Gracious Father, help me to serve You and to see the opportunities You give me to love others. Thank You for entrusting me with valuable resources to build Your kingdom as I share the love and message of Jesus. Amen.

Matthew 25:31-36

"When the Son of Man comes in his glory, and all the angels with him, he will sit on his glorious throne. All the nations will be gathered before him, and he will separate the people one from another as a shepherd separates the sheep from the goats. He will put the sheep on his right and the goats on his left.

"Then the King will say to those on his right, 'Come, you who are blessed by my Father; take your inheritance, the kingdom prepared for you since the creation of the world. For I was hungry and you gave me something to eat, I was thirsty and you gave me something to drink, I was a stranger and you invited me in, I needed clothes and you clothed me, I was sick and you looked after me, I was in prison and you came to visit me.'" ...

This passage isn't like other parables Jesus told. He left no ambiguity here about his topic or thesis. He said straight out what He was about to describe. One day, He will come in glory with the heavenly host and sit on his throne to divide people into two categories. It will be like a shepherd separating sheep and goats. That's when the parable begins, but there's no mistaking that Jesus is telling us about something very real that will happen when He returns. There are a number of things that make this parable challenging for us. As we read further, we will need to address what the parable teaches about salvation and the necessity of good works, but for now let's focus on the challenging idea of Jesus separating humanity into two distinct groups. Sheep and goats. Good and bad. Worthy and unworthy.

We struggle with the notion of drawing lines of division between people because, well, who am I to judge? I know I'm a sinner and am not worthy of God's unending love. While I may look down on the sins of others, I need to be careful not to condemn someone else for the same sin that I commit. Maybe it's easy to pick out some of the goats, the really bad people who do terrible things, but most people's lives seem more grey than black or white, sort of good and sort of bad all mixed together. So, how am I supposed to tell the difference between the sheep and the goats? Here's the thing: that's not my job, and it's not yours either. Jesus is the only one who will sit on that throne and do the work of separating.

Our calling is not to play judge or jury over the lives of others. No, our calling is to live out genuine faith by doing the things the King witnessed his good sheep doing. Feed the hungry. Give refreshing water to the thirsty. Welcome strangers. Clothe those in need. Care for the sick. Visit the outcast and imprisoned. Those are things good sheep do in service to their King. Those are things Jesus' followers do to bring honor to his name. One day, Jesus will return and do his promised work of separating sheep and goats, and until then, we know exactly the type of things Jesus wants his sheep to do.

Father in Heaven, You are good and wise. Thank You for the promise that Jesus will return. May that day come soon! For now, help me to love others in Your name and to share with them the good news of salvation through Jesus. I pray in His name. Amen.

Matthew 25:37-40

"Then the righteous will answer him, 'Lord, when did we see you hungry and feed you, or thirsty and give you something to drink? When did we see you a stranger and invite you in, or needing clothes and clothe you? When did we see you sick or in prison and go to visit you?'
"The King will reply, 'Truly I tell you, whatever you did for one of the least of these brothers and sisters of mine, you did for me.'" ...

If you see a young man wearing shoulder pads and a helmet, you might assume that he is a football player. He might look strong and tough, and he might be wearing a jersey with the name of a well-known team. He might even talk about what position he plays and how much experience he has on the gridiron. As you look at him and listen to him talk, you might become convinced that he really is a football player, but it's not until he actually runs onto the field and lines-up with his team that you can know for sure that he is what he claims to be.

Jesus didn't tell this parable to explain how someone becomes a Christian or what qualifies us to get into heaven. He told it to motivate his followers to actually live out, through word and deed, what we claim to be. We are saved by grace through faith in Jesus. This parable doesn't teach some other type of salvation based on how many good deeds we do, but Jesus wants us to know that a person of genuine faith, whose heart has been deeply and forever changed by God's grace, will do good deeds in Jesus' name. We will love people in need as a way of loving our Lord. We will care for the sick, the poor and the imprisoned as though we were caring for Jesus himself. These good things we do don't save our souls, but they give evidence that our souls have been saved by grace.

All too often we put on a jersey and shoulder pads without actually lining up to run a play on the field. We talk about faith, sing joyful songs and read the Bible in quiet devotional times, but how often do we turn our faith into actions of love, compassion and self-giving service? What I like best about this parable is the humility of the righteous people who are surprised to hear that their acts of kindness have been noticed by the King. They do good things out of the goodness of their hearts, not realizing that by loving others they are in fact loving their King. May we love the same way, not to be noticed or praised or because we are trying to earn God's favor, but because Jesus has changed our hearts so much that loving people has become who we actually are.

Jesus, teach me to love others the way You love me. Show me how to give to those in need and how to lift up those who are struggling. Use me to spread Your goodness and grace in this broken, hurting world. I ask this in Your wonderful name. Amen.

Matthew 25:41-46

"Then he will say to those on his left, 'Depart from me, you who are cursed, into the eternal fire prepared for the devil and his angels. For I was hungry and you gave me nothing to eat, I was thirsty and you gave me nothing to drink, I was a stranger and you did not invite me in, I needed clothes and you did not clothe me, I was sick and in prison and you did not look after me.'

"They also will answer, 'Lord, when did we see you hungry or thirsty or a stranger or needing clothes or sick or in prison, and did not help you?'

"He will reply, 'Truly I tell you, whatever you did not do for one of the least of these, you did not do for me.'

"Then they will go away to eternal punishment, but the righteous to eternal life."

Jesus said a lot of hard things, and these words may be the hardest of all. He seems to be telling us that some people will reach the Judgment believing they are good, faithful people only to be condemned to eternal punishment for failing to show enough love to people in need. Could that happen to me? Could I miss out on heaven because I didn't care for a stranger?

On one hand, Jesus' words should motivate us to love well, to care for people in need and to show compassion to those who suffer, because in doing so, we prove the genuineness of our faith and express love for Jesus. Don't discount the challenging, motivating aspect of this parable, especially with so much hardship and suffering in our world. On the other hand, we know from the wider counsel of scripture that salvation is a matter of God's grace and our faith. You are not saved because you are good enough or because of the quantity of your loving compassion toward other people. You might be a kind person, but no one is good enough to earn her way to heaven, much less atone for his own sin. Jesus died on the cross exactly because we aren't good enough, precisely because none of us will live up to the standard of perfect love to which God calls us.

So, where does that leave us? What do we do with this parable? First, we don't ignore it. We don't say that love and compassion aren't really required of Jesus' followers. Instead, we embrace the calling of Jesus' words. We set our hearts on loving as well and as often and as generously as we can. We love family and friends, neighbors and strangers, people like us and people not like us. We love people as though they were Jesus himself. And for the times we fall short, we fall on God's grace. My guess is that when we stand before the judgment seat of God, there will be plenty of surprises. We may be shocked by just how sinful and selfish our lives have been and by how desperately we need God's grace. We may also be amazed by how many little acts of kindness God noticed in our lives and by how deeply Jesus changed our hearts to reflect his goodness.

Thank You, Lord, for showing me perfect love and for calling me to share Your love with others. Forgive me for all the ways I fail to love perfectly. Help me to be more like Jesus. Amen.

Mark 4:21-23

He said to them, "Do you bring in a lamp to put it under a bowl or a bed? Instead, don't you put it on its stand? For whatever is hidden is meant to be disclosed, and whatever is concealed is meant to be brought out into the open. If anyone has ears to hear, let them hear."

One of the surest signs of a cult or false religion is how often its leaders put lamps under bowls. Cults operate in secret, and they keep secrets even from their own followers. Any religion or ideological movement that doesn't trust people with the ideas they are supposed to believe shouldn't be trusted by anyone. Our faith has no secrets. Jesus came to disclose truth and to proclaim good news and to shed light on the wonderful wisdom of God. He put the lamp of the gospel high a stand for all to see, and He expects his followers to do the same.

It's tempting to hide who we are and what we believe. After all, the world doesn't always like Christians. Those who live in darkness often resent the light. That's why, when we put the lamp of our faith on a stand, we need to do so in love. Letting your light shine before others shouldn't be a way to judge or criticize, nor should it be done to make yourself look holy. Instead, we disclose the truth and wisdom of God for the sake of helping others and as a way to show love to those in need. We believe God's word and the message of Jesus is actually good news that brings people encouragement, hope and joy. Yes, some will reject our message. Some will hide from the light or even try to cover it up, but our calling is to bring the good news out into the open where it can cut through darkness and guide those seeking truth to new life.

We may also face the temptation to shine light into people's eyes in a way that blinds them to the truth. When someone has spent all their life in the dark, it can be shocking, even painful, to suddenly see a flash of light. Sometimes, we might push too hard or share our faith with so much enthusiasm that it sounds too good to be true. Some people need time to let their eyes adjust to the light and to let their hearts adjust to the good news of Jesus. We put his light on a stand and let it shine all around, trusting that the Spirit will open the eyes and hearts of those ready to put their faith in Jesus.

Father, the light of Your truth has saved me from darkness. Thank You for leading me to new life through the good news of Jesus. Show me how I can spread Your light to others, so they can find life in Jesus' name too. Amen.

Mark 4:26-29

He also said, "This is what the kingdom of God is like. A man scatters seed on the ground. Night and day, whether he sleeps or gets up, the seed sprouts and grows, though he does not know how. All by itself the soil produces grain – first the stalk, then the head, then the full kernel in the head. As soon as the grain is ripe, he puts the sickle to it, because the harvest has come."

You and I can't save anyone. We can't make someone believe in Jesus. We can't love them enough or convince them with clever words or force them to acknowledge that Jesus is Lord. Only the Holy Spirit can change someone's heart, just as the Spirit has changed our hearts. What we can do, though, is scatter seed on the ground. We can speak truth, share good news and tell people how Jesus has changed us. Those little seeds, maybe even words we have forgotten we said, can take root in someone's heart and, through the Spirit's power, can grow into faith.

This parable is sort of a follow-up to the parable of the soils. In that story, the farmer scatters seed onto various type of soil, some good for planting and others too rocky or hard or thorny for the seed to take root. In this parable, Jesus describes how a seed in good soil grows up into ripe grain ready for harvest. The farmer may not be able to explain how it grows and can't take credit for the amazing transformation that takes place as the seed sprouts up from the soil and grows into a fruitful stalk of grain. In fact, all the farmer does is scatter the seed. God does the hard work of turning that seed into a valuable harvest.

I know teachers who have run into former students, now grown and living productive lives, and been blessed to hear those students express appreciation for lessons taught and examples shown years before. Those teachers may not remember what they said to impact their students, but their words took root. In the same way, words of encouragement you speak and acts of love you show to others can reach deeply into their hearts to be used by God to change their lives. You may not know how it will happen or how long it will take, but keep scattering the good seed of God's love and trust that the Spirit will turn it into a harvest of eternal life.

Gracious Lord, Your word has changed my heart, and it can change the hearts of people I know. Use me to spread Jesus' message of hope. May Your Spirit continue to produce an abundant harvest of lives changed through Jesus the Savior. I ask this in His name. Amen.

Luke 6:46-49

"Why do you call me, 'Lord, Lord,' and do not do what I say? As for everyone who comes to me and hears my words and puts them into practice, I will show you what they are like. They are like a man building a house, who dug down deep and laid the foundation on rock. When a flood came, the torrent struck that house but could not shake it, because it was well built. But the one who hears my words and does not put them into practice is like a man who built a house on the ground without a foundation. The moment the torrent struck that house, it collapsed and its destruction was complete."

We are often tempted by shortcuts. They aren't always bad, of course. If your GPS suggests a route you have never tried before, it might save a little time or a few extra miles. Navigational shortcuts are one thing, but when it comes to getting important things done, shortcuts are often just excuses to cut corners which can lead to real trouble. Especially if you are constructing a home. Even worse, if you are trying to build a strong, healthy spiritual life.

Jesus' story imagines two men building their homes. One takes the time to do it right, laying a strong foundation to stabilize his house. The other builder cuts corners, takes the easy way, thinks he knows a shortcut, and cares more about getting it done than getting it right. The collapse of the second man's house represents the lazy, shortcut-following life of someone who claims to know Jesus but doesn't do what He says. That sort of spiritual life is all too common and all too tragic. What Jesus wants, of course, is for us to take the time to dig down deep, to lay the foundation of our souls on the solid rock of knowing Jesus, listening to him and putting his words into practice.

It's hard to dig down deep. It requires careful planning, like reading God's word each day. It takes strong tools, like faithful prayer. It involves sweat and sore muscles, like the effort it takes to obey God's word, putting into practice the wisdom and teaching of Jesus. There are no shortcuts when it comes to following our Lord. Cutting corners in your spiritual life leads to disappointment and may result in the collapse of your faith. Instead, put in the hard work of obedience and spiritual devotion, and commit yourself to actions of love and service. A well-lived, deeply dug life will honor Jesus and will steady your heart against the torrents of trouble we all face.

God of Grace, help me to do what You want and to put into practice the wisdom of Jesus. Thank You for showing me grace when I need it and for allowing my life to rest secure on the firm foundation of Your love. I pray in my Savior's name. Amen.

Luke 10:30-32

In reply Jesus said: "A man was going down from Jerusalem to Jericho, when he was attacked by robbers. They stripped him of his clothes, beat him and went away, leaving him half dead. A priest happened to be going down the same road, and when he saw the man, he passed by on the other side. So too, a Levite, when he came to the place and saw him, passed by on the other side." ...

It's so easy to "pass by on the other side." Don't get involved. It's not your problem. You aren't responsible. How often do we look the other way so we don't have to witness suffering or injustice or sorrow? If we act like we don't see a hurting person then we can continue on our way without stepping into the messy business of helping. We do it when confronted with the injustice of racism: I'll just look the other way… it's not my fault… I'm not responsible. Or what about the trauma of domestic violence: I'm not really sure what happened… that's their business… it's sad, but what can I do? And so, we pass by on the other side.

Jesus chose the characters in this story on purpose. The two people who pass by without helping the injured man are not just ordinary travelers; they are people who should know better than to leave someone to die on the side of the road. A priest and a Levite. A pastor and a church leader. Respected and responsible people. Of course, they aren't responsible for the man's injuries, but they become responsible for his care. The moment they see him bruised and bloody, stripped naked and left for dead, they are called by God to show compassion and, at the very least, to recognize the man's suffering. But instead, they pass by on the other side.

Why do we do things like that? Of course, there are times when we get it right, when we kneel down to help someone in need, but human history and each of our lives is littered with missed opportunities to love our neighbors in moments of need. Maybe we are afraid that what happened to them may happen to us. Maybe we are too stingy, too busy or too self-absorbed to care about a fellow human's life. Maybe we think those who suffer somehow deserve their fate, and we don't want to contaminate ourselves with whatever led to their troubles. Maybe it's just easier to pass by on the other side than to get involved. Maybe these excuses outweigh the compassion in our hearts when we hear of people suffering because of the color of their skin or when we see evidence of abuse or when we learn of a neighbor's financial hardship or when we witness any other sort of need. Jesus told this parable to cause people who think they lead good, God-fearing lives to rethink how we treat our neighbors before giving in to the temptation to pass by on the other side.

Father of Compassion, thank You for loving me more than I deserve and for lifting me up when I am in need. Teach me to love better. Fill my heart with compassion for those who are hurting so I can love the way Jesus asks me to. Amen.

Luke 10:33-35

"But a Samaritan, as he traveled, came where the man was; and when he saw him, he took pity on him. He went to him and bandaged his wounds, pouring on oil and wine. Then he put the man on his own donkey, brought him to an inn and took care of him. The next day he took out two denarii and gave them to the innkeeper. 'Look after him,' he said, 'and when I return, I will reimburse you for any extra expense you may have.'" ...

Wouldn't it be great if, when the world thought about Christians and the church, the first images in their minds were of selfless acts of compassion? I think Jesus would be pleased if the people called by his name were known best for love and service, like the Samaritan in this parable. Of course, many Christians do give of themselves in wonderfully loving ways. There are orphanages and homeless shelters run and funded by followers of Jesus. There are medical clinics and facilities that care for pregnant women and their children operated by people who serve in the name of Jesus. There are churches that reach out to their communities in sacrificial ways to lift up the hurting and care for those who suffer. Jesus' followers show compassion in many ways that the world may overlook or choose to ignore, but we also need to admit that we often fall short of loving as purely and as selflessly as Jesus wants us to.

The Samaritan in Jesus' parable gets love right from beginning to end. First, he sees the injured man and feels compassion for him. We know from the first part of this story (and from the experience of our own lives) that it's easy to look the other way when someone is in need, but the Samaritan sees the man, takes pity, and goes to care for him. He bandages the man's wounds, touching him with healing love. Then the Samaritan carries him from that desolate place to an inn where he can be tended to and watched overnight. He even pays for the man's care, promising to return and cover any additional expenses. What extraordinary compassion! What generous love!

Jesus told this story to show us what love looks like. It looks like hands that heal. It looks like time and expense given without complaint. It looks like carrying someone who can't carry himself. It looks like a promise to keep loving, far beyond obligation and to the point of full restoration. That's the type of love Jesus shows us. He came into our world with healing power and compassion for those who suffer. He walked alongside broken people, giving them hope by pointing them toward a better life. He gave up his own life to save us, offering us the greatest gift of love the world has ever known. Now, Jesus calls us to love others in his name, and when we do, the world catches a glimpse of God's compassionate heart.

Lord, You are perfect in love and full of mercy toward people in need. Thank You for seeing my needs and lifting me up. Show me how I can spread Your love to others and offer compassion in Jesus' name. Amen.

Luke 10:36-37

"Which of these three do you think was a neighbor to the man who fell into the hands of robbers?"
The expert in the law replied, "The one who had mercy on him."
Jesus told him, "Go and do likewise."

This epilogue to the parable of the good Samaritan teaches us three surprising truths. First, Jesus' question turned the thinking of the expert in the law upside down in a way that should reshape our thinking too. The expert had asked, "Who is my neighbor?" by which he meant, who am I required to love? He wanted Jesus to draw a circle around those we have to love, so we can then withhold love from everyone else. Jesus' question flipped it around, asking instead, who acted like a neighbor to the man in need? In other words, the Samaritan chose to become the injured man's neighbor out of a compassionate heart, not because someone said he had to. Jesus wants to expand our circle of neighbors.

The second truth has to do with qualities of the heart. What does it mean that the expert in the law identified the good neighbor not as "the Samaritan" but as "the one who had mercy"? Jesus chose to make the hero of his story a Samaritan, a person from an ethnic group routinely marginalized by the majority Jewish population. Jesus did this, it's safe to say, to push back against prejudice and to emphasize his conviction that anyone and everyone can be your neighbor. The expert in the law, touched by Jesus' story, referred to the Samaritan according to his humanity and the goodness of his heart. He was not just a foreigner or an outsider or an ethnic minority. He was "one who had mercy." He chose to be a neighbor to someone in need and was therefore judged "by the content of [his] character," to quote Martin Luther King, Jr.

The third truth is less surprising than it is challenging. Jesus tells us to "go and do likewise." That sounds like something Jesus would have said often at the end of his sermons and parables, but this passage is the only time in the Gospels where Jesus used this phrase. And He meant it. Go and be a loving, merciful neighbor. Don't pass by on the other side. Don't split hairs over who is and who is not your neighbor. Don't refuse mercy to people who look different or speak different. Love. Show mercy. Give compassion. Be like Jesus to those in need.

Father of Mercy, teach me how to love. Lead me to people in need, and fill my heart with mercy so I can extend to them the love of Jesus my Savior. Amen.

Luke 14:15-17

When one of those at the table with him heard this, he said to Jesus, "Blessed is the one who will eat at the feast in the kingdom of God."

Jesus replied: "A certain man was preparing a great banquet and invited many guests. At the time of the banquet he sent his servant to tell those who had been invited, 'Come, for everything is now ready.'" ...

I don't think I've ever been to a real banquet. I've attended large dinners in hotel conference rooms and a few nice wedding receptions, but not a great banquet like the one Jesus' story imagines. Banquets feature extravagant decorations and delicious food served in several courses. People attend banquets to celebrate big, important moments. The banquet hall should be filled with a large, joyful crowd. I suppose some banquets could be formal, like a White House state dinner, while others are fun and festive, like the lavish affairs of The Great Gatsby. I think the banquet Jesus had in mind would be a party and a feast and a celebration all rolled into one.

Of course, Jesus' parable points us heavenward to the grand celebration we will enjoy in God's presence, the great feast Jesus will host for all his faithful followers. As we continue reading the parable, we will learn about the invited guests and their attitudes toward the banquet, but for now, let's enjoy imagining what it will be like to sit down at that enormous table with brothers and sisters in faith from every nation, tribe, people and language. The food will come from the magnificent abundance of heaven, perfectly delicious for our heavenly bodies and good for our imperishable souls. We will sing praise to God and declare his glories and goodness. We will share stories of miracles, answered prayers, spiritual transformations and the Spirit's power flowing through God's people. And our host, Jesus himself, will embrace each of us with grace, assuring us that this celebration will never end.

It's good for us to think about heaven. Jesus talked about it all the time, and so should we. His invitation to the great banquet is the invitation to eternal life, and while we have important work to do here and now – like sharing this invitation with others – we should also rejoice in the hope of joining the heavenly celebration. When life is hard we should look ahead with faithful expectation to the beauty of heaven. When we feel stressed by the brokenness of this world, we should anticipate the perfection that awaits us. We should remember Jesus' invitation to the great banquet and give thanks.

Thank You, Father, for inviting me to heaven. I rejoice in Your goodness and wait with great hope for that everlasting time of celebration and praise. May Your banquet hall be filled with multitudes of faithful people who have found eternal life in Jesus. Amen.

Luke 14:18-20

"But they all alike began to make excuses. The first said, 'I have just bought a field, and I must go and see it. Please excuse me.'

"Another said, 'I have just bought five yoke of oxen, and I'm on my way to try them out. Please excuse me.'

"Still another said, 'I just got married, so I can't come.'" ...

You may have heard it said, if you want to know what you value most in life, take a look at your bank statement or your credit card bill. I suppose you could also learn a good deal about yourself by looking back at your calendar. Where have you chosen to go and who have you spent time with? What do the appointments you make and the commitments you keep say about the condition of your heart? Of course, there are things we have to do that we may not want to do, but in many ways, our lives are defined by the things we say "yes" to versus the things we say "no" to.

Jesus' parable is about making excuses. In one sense, Jesus is talking about people who reject him because they care more about things in this world than the eternal things Jesus offers. People make excuses instead of opening their hearts to faith. Then again, I think Jesus also wants his followers to consider how often we make excuses to get out of doing things He asks us to do. In that sense, the parable calls us to examine our values and priorities. What comes first in your life? What matters most and takes precedence over everything else? If Jesus were to invite you to dinner, would you make excuses or would you drop everything and rearrange your schedule to make sure you were at that dinner?

It's striking that the excuses each person makes in the parable sound like valid, legitimate reasons not to attend a banquet. These people have commitments. They are being responsible. They are busy doing good things and believe that their work and relationships matter more than going to a party.

We might even agree with their decisions to reject the invitation, until we remember that this banquet stands for eternal life and it's God who sends out the invitations. Nothing in this life, not even family and career obligations, should matter more to us than our relationship with God. He must always come first. His invitations should always get top billing in our hearts. To be clear, God calls us to care for our families, love our neighbors, work hard and be active in our communities. That is, we can honor God by doing the very things that often fill our calendars. But we need to be sure we are doing them to honor God and not as ways to look too busy or to feel too important to join the banquet of eternal life.

Father in Heaven, You come first in my life. Forgive me for the times I make excuses for not putting You first. Loving You and honoring Jesus matter more to me than any other commitment I have made. Help me to live that way today, in Jesus' name. Amen.

Luke 14:21-24

"The servant came back and reported this to his master. Then the owner of the house became angry and ordered his servant, 'Go out quickly into the streets and alleys of the town and bring in the poor, the crippled, the blind and the lame.'

"'Sir,' the servant said, 'what you ordered has been done, but there is still room.'

"Then the master told his servant, 'Go out to the roads and country lanes and compel them to come in, so that my house will be full. I tell you, not one of those who were invited will get a taste of my banquet.'"

This parable seems to ring two bells at the same time. One sounds like a warning siren, cautioning those who haven't joined the Kingdom. The other is the joyful ring of a dinner bell, inviting all who hear it to gather for the banquet of life. Jesus wants everyone to hear both bells, to take the warning to heart and to know beyond doubt that we have been invited to the Kingdom feast. Bells get our attention by breaking through the ordinary noise around us, calling us to stop, look and consider the meaning of the alarm. What is Jesus saying to us? Is He talking to me? Do I need to give heed to his warning or make sure I have accepted his gracious invitation?

The master in Jesus' parable, representing God, wants his house to be full of those eager to receive his hospitality and joyful to celebrate at his feast. That is God's heart, isn't it? He loves to love us. He longs to welcome us. He wants his house to be full. God created this enormous, amazingly intricate world to give us a place where we can know and love him. In that sense, God is our host in this life, having designed this world just for us, and if that weren't enough, He also longs to host us at the grand banquet of eternity. In fact, God wants us at that heavenly celebration so much that He sent Jesus to die and rise again so we could be declared worthy to enter his holy presence. God really, really loves you and really, really wants you to be with him forever.

But He won't force anyone to accept his invitation. God also created this world, in a metaphysical sense, to give us a choice, free will to love him or to reject him. Some people hear the good news of Jesus, understand that He offers them everlasting life, even taste the graciousness of God's provision, and then still turn away to pursue the fleeting, failing things of this world. They make excuses or raise objections or simply grab for the immediate gratification of earthly pleasures, rather than bow their hearts to the Savior who offers the only way to eternal joy and salvation. We grieve, along with God, for those who reject Jesus' invitation to life, and we rejoice with our brothers and sisters who, by faith, have accepted that invitation and will join us for the heavenly banquet.

Father, You are glorious and gracious. Thank you for inviting me to know You and to be with You for eternity. I love You, and I hold fast to the hope of entering Your wonderful presence, through Jesus my Savior. Amen.

Luke 15:11-12

Jesus continued: "There was a man who had two sons. The younger one said to his father, 'Father, give me my share of the estate.' So he divided his property between them." ...

We all enter the world selfish and demanding. You may not remember your own infancy, but if you are a parent or have ever cared for a baby, even for a few hours, you know that young children think only of their own needs. Of course, we don't blame babies for crying when they are hungry or tired or uncomfortable. We don't expect newborns to help out around the house or pick up after themselves. They are too young. They haven't grown up into the maturity that should bring compassion for others and a sense of responsibility for the people and things around them. As we develop, learn and grow, we come to understand that we not only need other people, but that they also need us and that it's good to share, give, serve and love. Sadly, there also remains in each of us embers of those selfish desires, and sometimes they ignite again into fires of greedy self-centeredness.

That is the younger son's disease: at his core, the young man at the center of Jesus' parable has put himself at the center of life with everything and everyone else orbiting around his wants and wishes. So self-focused is this young man that he doesn't hesitate to tell his father, in essence, "Drop dead and give me what I have coming." Maybe he doesn't really think through his request that profoundly. All he seems concerned with is getting his hands on his share of his estate and doing whatever he desires with his property, that is with the property that has been, up until his outrageous request, his father's hard-earned wealth. These opening lines to Jesus' best-known parable were meant to cause immediate indignation in his listeners' hearts, because they would understand, as we also should, just how offensively self-centered the young man is.

Jesus knows how to strike chords in our hearts, some beautiful and stirring, others shrill and jarring. It may hurt, but we need to hear the moral and spiritual dissonance of the young man's request and to recognize how often we also play self-centered tunes. I want... I need... I think... If I were in charge... Those notes rarely harmonize with love, compassion and service. May we grow in maturity, putting aside selfish desires and greedy cravings, choosing instead to care well for others, just as Jesus cares for us.

Good Father, thank You for loving me more than I deserve. Please forgive all my self-centered words and actions. Teach me humility and compassion for others, so I can become more like Jesus, in whose name I pray. Amen.

Luke 15:13-16

"Not long after that, the younger son got together all he had, set off for a distant country and there squandered his wealth in wild living. After he had spent everything, there was a severe famine in that whole country, and he began to be in need. So he went and hired himself out to a citizen of that country, who sent him to his fields to feed pigs. He longed to fill his stomach with the pods that the pigs were eating, but no one gave him anything." ...

How often do we think, "She's getting what she deserves!" We look at the poor choices others make, as we sit comfortably at a safe, uninvolved distance, passing heartless judgments on those who suffer the predictable consequences of their reckless lives. Sometimes, we even enjoy witnessing the misfortune of the careless and the downfall of the foolish. The overdosed junkie. The pregnant teenager. The two-bit criminal whose mugshot splashes across the local news. Too bad. Oh well. Getting what they deserve, I suppose.

That's just what Jesus wants us to think at this point in the story. The younger son, after demanding his share of the family estate and flushing it away on parties and prostitutes, has to grovel in the mud with pigs, starving and pathetic. Good riddance to the good-for-nothing young man. Jesus wants us to think those heartless thoughts because that really is how we look at the downfall of others, and if we can be really honest, that's how we hope God looks at those sorts of people too. Shouldn't a just and fair God punish sinners and send hardship on fools? That's the sort of divine retribution we can understand and applaud, and Jesus knows we all have a cruel corner in our hearts that enjoys watching bad people get what they've got coming.

Without giving away the rest of the parable, you should know that this story is about grace and that, while we can identify with each of the three main characters, Jesus wants us first and foremost to see ourselves in the younger son. It's easy to cheer for justice to be meted out against others whose sins we consider so gross, but when we catch a glimpse of our own faults, when we see in ourselves the same sort of foolishness that we have condemned in others, we may start to reconsider the cold reality of strict justice. When we stand accused, we don't want to get what we deserve. That's when we give thanks for God's grace that saves sinners like us, grace that can even save people who squander their lives in wild living and find themselves in the mud with no one to give them anything, except our gracious God and Father.

Father of Mercy and Grace, You lifted me out of the mud of sin and hopelessness. You gave me new life through Jesus. Teach me to see others through Your gracious eyes and to join Jesus in offering hope and salvation to people in need. I pray in my Savior's name. Amen.

Luke 15:17-20

"When he came to his senses, he said, 'How many of my father's hired servants have food to spare, and here I am starving to death! I will set out and go back to my father and say to him: Father, I have sinned against heaven and against you. I am no longer worthy to be called your son; make me like one of your hired servants.' So he got up and went to his father.

"But while he was still a long way off, his father saw him and was filled with compassion for him; he ran to his son, threw his arms around him and kissed him." ...

The turning point of Jesus' parable depicts two resolutions of the heart. The first resolution must take place deep inside people like us, and the second comes from God's heart. First, we need to repent. That's what the young man does, lying in the pigsty with an empty stomach. He comes to his senses. He wakes up to the sad reality of his broken life. He decides that something deep in his heart must change. So, he repents, turning away from the loose and fast life that led to his despair and turning toward home. It's tragic that it often takes hitting rock bottom before some people will repent. It may take an overdose or getting caught cheating or spending the night in jail for driving drunk or some other shameful experience like the one suffered by the young man in Jesus' story. How much better it is for us to repent before we crash and burn.

Then comes God's part. God offers repentant sinners grace. Don't miss the vivid details in Jesus' description of the father embracing his long lost son, and as you consider these details, remember that Jesus was sent into this world by his own Heavenly Father for exactly this purpose: to offer grace to sinners who want to come home. The father, scanning the horizon with hope and expectation, sees his son coming from a long way off. His first reaction is not anger, resentment, or even relief. No, he is filled with compassion. The father runs to his son, casting off social proprieties in this outpouring of merciful love. And then, without waiting for explanation or apology, the father embraces and kisses his child. Jesus painted this portrait of grace to reflect the loving heart of our Heavenly Father.

We also shouldn't miss how quickly and shockingly the story turns. In the opening lines, Jesus draws our focus to the callous, self-centered depravity of the young man. We are sickened by his words and actions, to the point that we enjoy hearing of his lowly state of desperation as he wallows with the pigs. He's getting what he deserves! But then, suddenly, there goes the father, running and embracing his wayward son, erasing all his folly in an astonishing gesture of grace. This too reflects God's heart. Surprisingly merciful. Shockingly loving. Amazingly gracious.

Thank You, Father, for showing me grace and welcoming me home to Your loving arms. Help me to repent of all my sin and to find joy and hope in Your love alone. I pray in Jesus' good name. Amen.

Luke 15:21-24

"The son said to him, 'Father, I have sinned against heaven and against you. I am no longer worthy to be called your son.'

"But the father said to his servants, 'Quick! Bring the best robe and put it on him. Put a ring on his finger and sandals on his feet. Bring the fattened calf and kill it. Let's have a feast and celebrate. For this son of mine was dead and is alive again; he was lost and is found.' So they began to celebrate." ...

If you are a parent, I imagine you can easily identify with the father's joy at welcoming home his long, lost son. Most parents would be overjoyed to celebrate the return of a son or daughter, even a "prodigal" (that is, reckless or wasteful) child. But we know that the father in Jesus' parable is meant to represent God, so we must be called to identify ourselves with another character in the story. We must be like the wayward young man who laments, "I am no longer worthy to be called your son." Those words cut our hearts a little more deeply than we would like. Do you consider yourself unworthy? Unworthy of what? Love? Acceptance by God? A place in heaven? And if so, why? Surely, you haven't done as many terrible things as the son in Jesus' story. You haven't wished your parents dead and run away from home. You haven't wasted your family's fortune on wild living. The prodigal son may not be worthy to be called his father's son, but does the same go for you and me?

The sobering truth is that when Jesus told this parable, He had us in mind. When the foolish young man declares that he has sinned against heaven, Jesus was thinking about our sin. And when Jesus chose the words "not worthy," He was speaking a hard but undeniable truth about you and me. Yes, Jesus believes you are unworthy of God's embrace. He rightly considers you unfit for God's glorious presence. He knows you don't belong in heaven. That could have been the end of the story and the final judgment over our souls. We are prodigal, sinful, selfish, foolish people who don't deserve anything good from the God we so often disobey, dishonor and disgrace. And yet, that isn't the end of Jesus' story or of the Gospel. Jesus came to save us, not because we are worthy of salvation, but because in God's gracious heart, He chooses to declare us worthy of being welcomed home, of being loved as his dear children and of being celebrated in heaven above. God calls us worthy, according to his grace and because Jesus died for our sins.

The young son is struck dumb by his father's mercy; he doesn't speak another word in the parable. Hopefully, we can use our tongues to give thanks and praise to God for his overflowing grace. Hopefully, our hearts have been so deeply moved by God's mercy that we will turn away from our sinful desires and choose more and more to honor our Father. Hopefully, we will remember our unworthiness and never take for granted what Jesus suffered on our behalf.

Gracious Father, I am unworthy of Your love, and I rejoice in the good news that Jesus is my Savior. Thank You for taking away my sin and for giving me the great hope of being welcomed home to Your glorious presence. Through Jesus I pray. Amen.

Luke 15:25-30

"Meanwhile, the older son was in the field. When he came near the house, he heard music and dancing. So he called one of the servants and asked him what was going on. 'Your brother has come,' he replied, 'and your father has killed the fattened calf because he has him back safe and sound.'

"The older brother became angry and refused to go in. So his father went out and pleaded with him. But he answered his father, 'Look! All these years I've been slaving for you and never disobeyed your orders. Yet you never gave me even a young goat so I could celebrate with my friends. But when this son of yours who has squandered your property with prostitutes comes home, you kill the fattened calf for him!'" ...

What is the older brother feeling at this point in the story? Perhaps we could call it jealousy or envy, but I think it has more to do with that feeling we get when things aren't fair. How many times in your childhood did you cry about being treated unfairly by a parent or a teacher or by some other kid who you probably stopped being friends with because he gave someone else more than he gave you? We have highly sensitive fairness receptors, especially when a perceived injustice is perpetrated against us. When we get short-changed or slighted in even the most trivial ways, indignation immediately boils over our hearts and erupts in attitudes, words and actions meant to defend our honor against unfair treatment.

Jesus included this unexpected twist in his parable because He knows the human heart. The older brother represents good, faithful people like you and me, people who follow Jesus, do our best to obey God's word, keep ourselves from notorious sin and generally look down on people who act like the younger son in his lustful, reckless behavior. All the older brother wants is justice, fairness. He wants his little brother to be held accountable for his prodigal ways. Sin should be punished, and faithful service should be rewarded.

That's all he wants, and that's what we want too when we see bad people doing bad things. They should suffer the just consequences of their actions, and we should be celebrated for all the good we do. Anything less just isn't fair.

You might want to sit down for this next part. Jesus offers people grace, and grace isn't fair. In fact, grace turns fairness upside-down, treating sinners with mercy instead of wrath. We love to sing about God's grace when it flows over our lives, over our sin, but when God forgives someone else for their rotten, dirty transgressions, we turn into the older son who refuses to celebrate his brother's homecoming. Maybe it's pride or jealousy or just plain meanness, but we are often slow to rejoice in the grace God shows other sinners. The good news is that while grace isn't fair, God never runs out of it. He can pour grace over your sin and my sin and still have plenty left to cover the sins of everyone else who comes home to his loving embrace.

Father, I will never understand the mystery of Your grace, but I rejoice that my sins have been washed away through Jesus. Help me also to rejoice when You offer grace to others. I ask this in my Savior's name. Amen.

Luke 15:31-32

"'My son,' the father said, 'you are always with me, and everything I have is yours. But we had to celebrate and be glad, because this brother of yours was dead and is alive again; he was lost and is found.'"

If someone were to ask you to describe God, to explain what you think He is like, this parable may be the best place to start. In fact, if Jesus had been asked to illustrate God's character and essential nature, He may have told this story. The father, who graciously welcomes home his wayward son and who patiently draws his older child into the celebration, beautifully exemplifies the compassionate, merciful heart of God, who sent Jesus into the world to seek and save the lost. Not only does God want to save sinners and give new life to those who are dead in transgressions, the God of Grace also celebrates each transformed life. God is glad whenever a sinner comes home.

The touching beauty and profound theology of this parable remind us why Jesus told stories. His parables communicate truth, and at the same time, they reach into our souls where we are able, often beyond intellectual comprehension, to feel God's glory and goodness. We may struggle to explain why or how God can forgive our sins or what it means to be "born again," but when we hear this story of the merciful father celebrating his son's return, our hearts understand God. We can taste his gracious love. We feel his compassionate embrace. We grasp his unfathomable kindness, and it takes hold of us in the joyful gift of new life.

Let's not forget, these closing words are spoken to the older son, who had at first resented his father's mercy toward his brother, but is now invited to join the celebration. In the same way, we who know Jesus as our Savior need to ready our hearts to celebrate the redemption of other sinners. As we see the glad heart of God, we need also to be glad and to join with

Jesus in telling the world about our gracious God. Too many people believe, in part because of the church's failings and mixed messages, that God is vengeful, angry and merciless. Jesus calls us to join him in sharing good news, the joyful proclamation that God loves people and longs to welcome them home with a glad and gracious heart.

Thank You, Jesus, for teaching me who God is and how much He loves me. Help me to share this wonderful truth with others so they can find new life in Your name. I rejoice in Your love for me, even as I love You. Amen.

Luke 16:19-24

"There was a rich man who was dressed in purple and fine linen and lived in luxury every day. At his gate was laid a beggar named Lazarus, covered with sores and longing to eat what fell from the rich man's table. Even the dogs came and licked his sores.

"The time came when the beggar died and the angels carried him to Abraham's side. The rich man also died and was buried. In Hades, where he was in torment, he looked up and saw Abraham far away, with Lazarus by his side. So he called to him, 'Father Abraham, have pity on me and send Lazarus to dip the tip of his finger in water and cool my tongue, because I am in agony in this fire.'" ...

They say you can't teach an old dog new tricks, and I suppose the same goes for the rich man in this parable who, even in the flames of hell, still thought he was better than Lazarus and should be served by the poor beggar. That's one of several peculiar twists in Jesus' story. Another is the ability for people in hell to communicate with those in heaven. I don't know that we should build an entire theology of the afterlife on one parable, but the fact that Jesus told this story at least indicates that those in heaven and hell are conscious of their own condition relative to that of others. In fact, from this parable we can conclude that heaven and hell are present realities and that those who die today enter the afterlife immediately. While it may give us pause to think about the torment of those in hell, we should rejoice in the promise that those who died in Christ pass instantly into God's glorious presence and the peace of heaven.

This parable also raises some confusion over how or why we gain salvation. Is Jesus telling us that all rich people who live in luxury during this life will end up suffering in Hades? Is He also suggesting that all those who suffer now will be granted a place in heaven? These notions may be appealing to some people as a sort of eternal redistribution of wealth, but we know from the larger counsel of scripture that salvation comes through faith and by grace, not according to our works or our financial status. Simply put, Jesus didn't tell this parable to teach how we are saved. Rather, this story is meant to develop a sense of urgency in the hearts of unbelievers to seek after God before it's too late and, as we will read later in the parable, to motivate believers to share the good news of Jesus, again, before it's too late.

Let's also not miss the simple fact that Jesus had a firm certainty about the afterlife. We may be tempted to doubt the reality of heaven or to wish that hell didn't exist. While the characters and dialogue in Jesus' story are fictional, like all his parables, Jesus presents heaven and hell as every bit as real as the road to Jericho in the parable of the good Samaritan or the farmer's field in the parable of the sower and the soils. We can know for sure, with as much certainty as faith produces in our hearts, that heaven is real and that all those who find new life in Jesus will enter that glorious place.

Father, thank You for the hope of heaven. I rejoice in the promise that one day I will see You face to face and will be safe from all the hardship of this world. For now, help me to lead a good life, to honor Jesus and to care for those in need around me. I ask this in my Savior's name. Amen.

Luke 16:25-26

"But Abraham replied, 'Son, remember that in your lifetime you received your good things, while Lazarus received bad things, but now he is comforted here and you are in agony. And besides all this, between us and you a great chasm has been set in place, so that those who want to go from here to you cannot, nor can anyone cross over from there to us.'" ...

This image of a great chasm separating those in heaven from those in hell may upset our hearts and might even cause us to feel a little depressed. How could a loving God cut people off from his glory and goodness for all eternity by digging this impassable canyon? Doesn't God have compassion on sinners? What about grace and mercy and forgiveness? Our hearts, especially those softened by the good news and love of Jesus, long for a way to cross that chasm and save those in hell from torment. It's right that we should feel that sense of sorrow for the lost. Truth is, that's exactly why Jesus told this parable. His story isn't meant to celebrate the chasm or ridicule those, like the rich man, who end up suffering apart from God. Jesus' story is a warning, a flashing sign pleading with unbelievers to repent before it's too late.

That may sound like the old-fashioned language of revivalist preachers, thumbing their Bibles and imploring the crowds, "Turn or burn!" The image of the great chasm has been used to scare people toward faith, and some evangelists use the fearful threat of hell as a way to push people into accepting Jesus. I certainly don't think Jesus meant for his words to be turned into messages of fear or manipulation, but we shouldn't ignore the reality behind this parable. Hell is real. There is a chasm of eternal separation that prevents those in hell from ever reaching heaven. Most importantly, how people respond to Jesus in this life, either accepting his offer of grace or rejecting it, determines their eternal destiny. Our soft hearts may quail at the notion of people going to hell, but Jesus' own words and many other passages of scripture confirm this hard truth.

Again, don't forget that Jesus told this story to draw people to new life in his name. He came to save sinners, not condemn them. He died on the cross to make possible our escape from the flames of hell. He commissioned his followers to go into all nations with the good news of salvation precisely because God wants to spare people from ending up on the wrong side of the great chasm. This parable should make us uncomfortable in a way that fuels our desire to share Jesus' love and message with those far from God so they too can find grace, forgiveness and the promise of heaven through Jesus the Savior.

Thank You, Jesus, for speaking hard truths and for offering sinners the way to salvation. You died for my sin, and I rejoice in the new life You give me. Help me to share Your good news in joyful, loving ways. I pray this in Your name and for Your glory. Amen.

Luke 16:27-31

"He answered, 'Then I beg you, father, send Lazarus to my family, for I have five brothers. Let him warn them, so that they will not also come to this place of torment.'

"Abraham replied, 'They have Moses and the Prophets; let them listen to them.'

"'No, father Abraham,' he said, 'but if someone from the dead goes to them, they will repent.'

"He said to him, 'If they do not listen to Moses and the Prophets, they will not be convinced even if someone rises from the dead.'"

Because we know the rest of the story of Jesus' life, death and resurrection, we know the closing lines to this unusual parable serve as a prophetic warning. Jesus understood that many people in his own Jewish culture were not living in faith and obedience to God's word, signified here as not listening to Moses and the Prophets. These people may have acted religious and fallen into the trap of self-righteousness, like the rich man who trusted in the luxuries of his wealth. Jesus pointed out, through the guise of his parable, that some who listened to his teaching were, in fact, not following scripture, not honoring God and therefore not prepared to respond faithfully to the Savior who would soon die and rise again.

With hearts of faith, we struggle to fathom how people could fail to be convinced by the testimony of someone who has risen from the dead. Jesus' resurrection is the lynchpin of our faith, the life-giving truth at the heart of the gospel. We rejoice in the Easter story as the heart and soul of our own lives. Those without faith, however, aren't moved by the resurrection. They might deny that it ever happened. They might dismiss it as religious myth. They might explain away its significance in numerous ways and end up in the same position of unbelief as those to whom Jesus told his story. Even if someone rises from the dead, some people won't believe.

We are left, then, with the desperate cry of the rich man, begging for someone to tell his family how they can escape his terrible fate. Warn them, please, before it's too late! We should take these words to heart, as we pray for family members, friends and neighbors who do not yet know Jesus as their Savior. We believe that Jesus is the only hope for salvation and the only way to eternal life. He died and rose again that we might live with God forever. That is the good news, and we join with Jesus in sharing his message of salvation with those in need.

Heavenly Father, fill me with the assurance of Your love and the steadfast hope of new life through Jesus. I believe in His resurrection and trust in Your promise that one day I will enter Your glory. As I rejoice in the grace You offer me, help me also to share Jesus' love and message with others. I pray in my Savior's name. Amen.

Luke 18:1-5

Then Jesus told his disciples a parable to show them that they should always pray and not give up. He said: "In a certain town there was a judge who neither feared God nor cared what people thought. And there was a widow in that town who kept coming to him with the plea, 'Grant me justice against my adversary.'

"For some time he refused. But finally he said to himself, 'Even though I don't fear God or care what people think, yet because this widow keeps bothering me, I will see that she gets justice, so that she won't eventually come and attack me!'" ...

You can look all through the Bible and never find where it says, "The squeaky wheel gets the grease." That old saying isn't in God's word, but this parable comes close to the same meaning. Let's be honest, it's kind of an odd bit of advice from Jesus. Does He mean that we should bother God, nagging him until we get what we want? Do our prayers annoy God, like a squeaking wheel or a rattling motor, into action? And, even more concerning, is Jesus saying that, like the judge in his story, God doesn't really care about us? No, of course not. We will find, in the concluding lines of the parable, that the judge is meant to teach us that even an uncaring person may grant a persistent request; therefore, how much more will our kind, loving God answer our prayers!

The challenge for us comes in those two little words: "always pray." That sounds great, really super-spiritual and highly-devotional, but most of us lead busy lives with responsibilities like family, work, church commitments and, occasionally, recreation. We aren't monks living in cloistered towers where all distractions and temptations have been removed so we can dedicate every waking moment to prayer. In fact, Jesus doesn't call many of his followers to that type of monastic discipleship. Jesus wants us to have families, jobs and friendships out in the world. So, how can He expect us to pray all the time? I think the key to understanding what it means to "always pray" comes in the next few words: "and not give up." We can't pray non-stop, but we can pray without giving up. We can pray with a persistent faith that God hears us and will answer. We can pray with a constant assurance of God's goodness. We can pray with a faith that doesn't give up, no matter how heavy the burden or how long the wait.

The judge in Jesus' story is unfaithful and unkind, and yet he eventually does a good thing for the persistent widow. How much more will our good God do for the people He loves! We pray to the God who created this world for us. We pray to the God who promised salvation to sinners. We pray to the God who sent his own Son to die for us. We pray to the God who raised Jesus to new life and who gives us everlasting life as well. It may feel at times like God isn't answering your prayer or that you are bothering him with the same request time after time, but in faith, you can be sure that God hears you, loves you and will provide for you in his perfect timing and according to his perfect will. So, keep praying without giving up.

Almighty God, I know You are good and that You hear my prayers. Give me faith to keep praying as I wait for Your reply. I trust You to bring me the good things You want me to have, through Jesus my Lord. Amen.

Luke 18:6-8

And the Lord said, "Listen to what the unjust judge says. And will not God bring about justice for his chosen ones, who cry out to him day and night? Will he keep putting them off? I tell you, he will see that they get justice, and quickly. However, when the Son of Man comes, will he find faith on the earth?"

After finishing his parable about the persistent widow and the unjust judge, Jesus offered a few words of interpretation, a quick commentary on his own story. Jesus said that God secures justice for his people so much more generously and quickly than the unjust judge. As we pray, we can trust in God's goodness, kindness and mercy. Jesus' words bring us encouragement and hope, but then He adds a final question that should linger in our hearts. Jesus wonders what He will find when He returns. Will He find people who pray persistently and faithfully? Or will He find people who demand things of God but don't actually trust in God's goodness?

Jesus is asking us this question. It takes the form of a rhetorical question, one that He didn't expect people to answer out loud, but it's really a prophetic question that invites us to look deeply into our hearts and discern the quality of our faith. In that sense, Jesus does expect an answer. In fact, He expects a commitment, a devotional response from each of us. If Jesus were to return today, what evidence of faith would He find in your life? Could He tell how much you trust in God by the choices you make each day, by how you use your time, by your relationships, by the words you speak and by the prayers you lift up? Would He see that when you pray, you wait on God's answer like the persistent widow who knew the judge was her only hope for justice? Or would He see that your trust in God is only half-hearted and that you depend more on your own strength, ingenuity and wealth?

Faith is what separates persistent prayer that God

honors from bothersome grumbling that God ignores. When we pray from faith-filled hearts, we not only ask God to help us, but we also wait on his reply. We stop searching desperately for our own solutions and cease giving attention to fears and worries. We pray with a faith that does not give up on the goodness of God. The widow knew the unjust judge was her only hope, so she kept asking him for justice. In faith, we declare that our gracious, wise, powerful God is our only hope, so we keep praying that He will provide, protect and bless. May Jesus find faith in our hearts and hear it in the words of our prayers.

Lord, You are good, and I trust in Your justice and mercy. Please fill my heart with faith. Hear my prayers and answer in the time and in the way You know is best. I pray with faith in Jesus my Savior. Amen.

Luke 18:9-14

To some who were confident of their own righteousness and looked down on everyone else, Jesus told this parable: "Two men went up to the temple to pray, one a Pharisee and the other a tax collector. The Pharisee stood by himself and prayed: 'God, I thank you that I am not like other people—robbers, evildoers, adulterers—or even like this tax collector. I fast twice a week and give a tenth of all I get.'

"But the tax collector stood at a distance. He would not even look up to heaven, but beat his breast and said, 'God, have mercy on me, a sinner.'

"I tell you that this man, rather than the other, went home justified before God. For all those who exalt themselves will be humbled, and those who humble themselves will be exalted."

It's one thing to be arrogant before other people; it's quite another level of audacity to be arrogant in the presence of God. Can you imagine coming before God with an air of belonging, with a sense that you and God stand as equals in judgment or authority over other, lesser beings? I doubt many people actually think of themselves as God's equals, but some sure act that way. Maybe we all do, sometimes. Any time we look down on others, diminishing their worth or belittling their struggles, we also lift ourselves up a little higher toward God. We like the feeling of sitting in the judgment seat, pointing fingers of blame and shame at poor, little sinners. We even pretend to play God sometimes, condemning people for their faults, while conveniently forgetting our own. For those of us who have lived under God's grace for a long time, it becomes easy to take grace for granted and to allow our hearts to forget just how wretchedly sinful we are and how utterly lost we would be if not for Jesus' redeeming blood.

The tax collector's prayer should be written in large print across our hearts. "God, have mercy on me, a sinner." These may sound like the words of a lost soul pleading for salvation, but they should also be the heartbeat and humble cry of each believer. Even after many years of knowing, following and loving Jesus, we remain sinners in need of mercy. We can be sure of our salvation, feel joyful in God's presence, and trust completely in the Lord's unfailing love. But we should never take that love for granted, and we should never exalt ourselves over others as though we deserve God's love and they do not. Those who exalt themselves will eventually be humbled, and those who humble themselves, before God and other people, will be exalted through the redeeming grace of Jesus, who alone can wash away our sin and give us the hope of eternity with God.

Our world desperately needs God's grace and the message of Jesus, and our world needs humble followers of Jesus who love the lost and help fellow sinners find their way home. Jesus wants his church to be filled with tax collectors, sinners and other lowly souls crying out for mercy. This world celebrates the powerful and the arrogant, but God's Kingdom welcomes the weak and the humble.

Jesus, You humbled Yourself, even unto death on a cross. Help me to walk in humility and to lift others up to You through love and service. I pray this in Your mighty name. Amen.

JESUS' DEATH AND RESURRECTION

Now, we turn to the story that defines our faith. Jesus came into this world to become our Savior, and He accomplished that great mission by dying and rising again. All four Gospels tell this sorrowful and wonderful story. We will focus on Matthew's account. Jesus went to the cross to save the world, choosing to suffer and die, knowing it was God's plan and the only way to rescue people from sin. Then He rose again to new life to lead into eternal life all those who place their faith in him. May these words change your heart as they help you consider why Jesus died, what it was like for him to suffer, and how glorious was his resurrection.

Matthew 26:6-13

While Jesus was in Bethany in the home of Simon the Leper, a woman came to him with an alabaster jar of very expensive perfume, which she poured on his head as he was reclining at the table.

When the disciples saw this, they were indignant. "Why this waste?" they asked. "This perfume could have been sold at a high price and the money given to the poor."

Aware of this, Jesus said to them, "Why are you bothering this woman? She has done a beautiful thing to me. The poor you will always have with you, but you will not always have me. When she poured this perfume on my body, she did it to prepare me for burial. Truly I tell you, wherever this gospel is preached throughout the world, what she has done will also be told, in memory of her."

Our world starves for beautiful things. So much ugliness, bitterness and brokenness surround us that we may have a hard time finding the few truly good, noble, beautiful things that happen. Of course, they do happen, sometimes. Neighbors care for neighbors. People generously offer help to those who are hurting. Parents sacrifice for their children. God's people gather to sing praise to the Savior and to declare the truth of his word. When beautiful things like these happen, don't miss them and don't take them for granted. Our hearts need the few glimmers of goodness we can find to cut through the darkness that engulfs so much of our world.

The disciples almost missed the beauty of this woman's act of love and worship. They were caught up in financial worries and the social stigma of a woman daring to interrupt their meal. Jesus quieted their indignation, calling her gift of perfume and devotion "a beautiful thing." Jesus not only appreciated her generous, humble act, but He prophesied that what she had done would always be remembered as part of his story. She anointed Jesus with expensive perfume, offering him a gift of honor and praise. Whether she understood or not, she also foreshadowed Jesus' death and burial. Just as He said, we still read her story today and are inspired to bring our own gift of generous devotion to our Lord.

What can you bring Jesus? What beautiful gift of worship or service can you offer him? You might bring a song of praise. You might give a sacrificial financial gift to help grow the Kingdom. You might show compassion in Jesus' name to someone in need. You might create something meaningful or useful that will inspire others to worship God. Whatever you feel led to bring Jesus, be assured that He will receive and appreciate the beautiful gift you offer.

Jesus, You are worthy of all my praise and service. I love You and want to bring You something beautiful by loving others, lifting up Your name in worship and obeying Your word. I pray in Your good and mighty name. Amen.

Matthew 26:26-30

While they were eating, Jesus took bread, and when he had given thanks, he broke it and gave it to his disciples, saying, "Take and eat; this is my body."

Then he took a cup, and when he had given thanks, he gave it to them, saying, "Drink from it, all of you. This is my blood of the covenant, which is poured out for many for the forgiveness of sins. I tell you, I will not drink from this fruit of the vine from now on until that day when I drink it new with you in my Father's kingdom."

When they had sung a hymn, they went out to the Mount of Olives.

There aren't many sacred things left in our world. Even those of us who spend a good deal of time around the church don't often think about places or things as being sacred, holy, or spiritually set apart. Our modern, sophisticated world doesn't leave room for what used to be known as "mystery," those spiritual aspects of life that we can't quantify but still believe to be real. Modern people like to see, touch and measure things, and when we can't, we try to explain them away. We also prefer things to be what they are, rather than letting one thing symbolize another. All of which puts the Communion meal squarely outside our comfort zone.

The truth is, it's always been that way. Ever since Jesus asked his disciples to remember him by eating a meal that stands for his body and blood, his followers have struggled to make sense of this sacred, mysterious, symbolic ritual. Early Christians were often ridiculed for gathering to eat Jesus' flesh and blood, which is a good reminder of the importance of clear Biblical teaching inside and outside the church. Jesus invited his followers to share the bread and cup as a sacred ritual of remembrance and participation. This sacrament calls us to remember why Jesus' body was broken and his blood shed, and it invites us to celebrate his resurrection. The meal also allows us to join with Jesus in his death, as we surrender our lives fully to him, dying to sin and rising again as those who have been redeemed.

That's a lot of sacred weight to put on a bite of bread and a sip of juice. That's how symbols work, though, and how anything in this world can be considered sacred. We take something common and allow it to stand for something extraordinary. Through prayer, blessing and faith, the simple act of eating and drinking joins us spiritually with Jesus, even in his atoning death. We don't believe the bread is Jesus' body in a material way, nor the juice his blood, but we do believe that eating the meal draws us into a sacred moment of communion with our Savior and with one another in the church. The bread and cup Jesus offers us remain like many aspects of our faith: beyond our ability to fully comprehend and yet real, true, powerful and sacred.

Thank You, Jesus, for giving Your church a way to remember what You did for us. Thank You for dying so I can be forgiven and for rising again so I can have the assurance of everlasting life. Give me faith that sees beyond the things of this world, so I can know You and serve You with my whole heart. Amen.

Matthew 26:31-34

Then Jesus told them, "This very night you will all fall away on account of me, for it is written:
"'I will strike the shepherd,
  and the sheep of the flock will be scattered.'
But after I have risen, I will go ahead of you into Galilee."
Peter replied, "Even if all fall away on account of you, I never will."
"Truly I tell you," Jesus answered, "this very night, before the rooster crows, you will disown me three times."

Mike Tyson famously said, "Everybody has a plan until they get punched in the face." He knows what he's talking about when it comes to boxing, and to be honest, these words of pugilistic wisdom can also apply to other parts of life. We all think we have what it takes. We'll pass the test and stand strong and come through when the chips are down. Especially when it comes to our faith, we want to believe we would never turn our backs on Jesus. I hope not, but Jesus' own disciples, his closest friends and most faithful followers, all fell away when Jesus needed them the most. Even Peter – brash and boastful, strong and determined – would face and fail the test. "I never will," Peter declared, but Jesus knew what was coming. When it all seemed to be falling apart around him, Peter disowned his Lord not once, not twice, but three times that fateful night.

Most of our sins, including the little ways we "disown" Jesus, seem far more subtle than what Peter did. We rarely sin publically. Many of us have never been called on to renounce our faith, and we hope we never would. Then again, we are all sinners. We hurt people and disobey God. Sometimes, we fail to do things we know we should do. We might walk away from opportunities to proclaim Jesus' name, maybe out of fear, like Peter, or just because we don't feel like getting involved. We hope we would never do what Peter did, but we all share that same weak nature that sometimes cracks under pressure.

But don't miss the gracious promise in Jesus' words. After telling the disciples that they would all fall away, Jesus said He would go ahead of them into Galilee. Those words are an invitation to come back to him in faith. After the resurrection, Jesus would be waiting for them to come home. That is God's grace. He knows we are sinners. Jesus knows what we have done in the past and what we will do in the future, and yet He calls us to himself with forgiveness, mercy and grace. You are going to get punched in the face again, and you are going to do things you will regret. You will fall into sin again, and Jesus will be there again to offer you forgiveness. The Risen Savior is going ahead of you so He can show you the way back to God's grace.

Father, You are full of grace and mercy. Thank You for sending Jesus to die for me so I can live forever with You. Forgive my sins and help me to be strong in the name of Jesus. Amen.

Matthew 26:36-39

Then Jesus went with his disciples to a place called Gethsemane, and he said to them, "Sit here while I go over there and pray." He took Peter and the two sons of Zebedee along with him, and he began to be sorrowful and troubled. Then he said to them, "My soul is overwhelmed with sorrow to the point of death. Stay here and keep watch with me."

Going a little farther, he fell with his face to the ground and prayed, "My Father, if it is possible, may this cup be taken from me. Yet not as I will, but as you will."

They say, "misery loves company," which usually means we might feel better about our own suffering if we know others are also going through tough times. In that sense, it's not a nice sentiment at all, like wishing misery on others just to make yourself feel better. Then again, it could point to a very different truth: we need friends around us when we are suffering. Jesus sure did. He asked his disciples to stay with him and "keep watch." He wanted their company during that miserable time of anticipating the cross. Jesus knew what cup He would soon have to drink, and his soul was "overwhelmed with sorrow."

This passage, perhaps more than any other in the Bible, displays Jesus' humanity. We believe He is fully God and that even during his time on earth He remained divine. And yet, He was also fully human for that time. He lived in a body like ours, with all its limitations, needs, weaknesses and pains. Jesus walked among us as a man, and He felt just what we would feel if we knew suffering and death were right around the corner. He didn't just act "troubled," He really was. That's why, in his great hour of need, Jesus asked his friends to stay with him. In that moment, He didn't want to be alone. Neither do we. Some burdens are too heavy to carry by ourselves, too difficult to bear. We need friends, family and the church to keep watch with us. We need their encouragement. We need their strength and faith and hope. We need their prayers.

Jesus taught us another lesson about prayer on that dark night. He submitted his will to God, even though it was hard. We can see the struggle between his human nature that wanted to avoid suffering and his determination to fulfill his mission to win salvation for the world through his atoning death. In the end, Jesus chose submission to God's will. It takes great faith to pray for God's will to be done. It means giving up control. It means surrendering to what God knows is best even when we don't know what that will mean for us. In faith, we believe God's will is good and perfect. He will accomplish in us what He knows is right. Jesus embraced God's will that night and taught us to do the same.

Father, I trust You to do what is best in my life. Give me courage to face what You know lies ahead, and surround me with friends who can lift me up when I am in need. Then use me to encourage and support others. I ask this in Jesus' name. Amen.

Matthew 27:27-31

Then the governor's soldiers took Jesus into the Praetorium and gathered the whole company of soldiers around him. They stripped him and put a scarlet robe on him, and then twisted together a crown of thorns and set it on his head. They put a staff in his right hand. Then they knelt in front of him and mocked him. "Hail, king of the Jews!" they said. They spit on him, and took the staff and struck him on the head again and again. After they had mocked him, they took off the robe and put his own clothes on him. Then they led him away to crucify him.

Sometimes we laugh at what we don't understand. The Roman soldiers who were assigned to prepare Jesus for crucifixion didn't know who He was. They had heard, maybe from their superiors, that this condemned man claimed to be the king of the Jews. They thought that was ridiculous, even funny, so they mocked him. Their tormenting words and cruel actions caused Jesus to suffer physically and emotionally. We may not enjoy reading this part of Jesus' story, but it is essential to understanding who He is. He came to suffer and to die for us, and his suffering was real. He felt the blows in his body. He felt the mockery in his heart.

We can't forget as we read these terrible verses that Jesus is God. The soldiers didn't understand that. They thought He was just a person, and they were trained to be cruel to people. What they did should never have been done to any person, even a guilty person justly sentenced by a legitimate court, but to do these things to Jesus, the incarnate Son of God and Savior of the world, is utterly shocking. That Jesus would allow them to treat him this way, to submissively accept their abuse and ridicule, is beyond our comprehension. How could people treat God's Son this way? How could God allow it to happen? It's hard to bear these truths, but this is what Jesus came to do. He was born to die. He came to give his life as a ransom for many (Mark 10:45). "While we were still sinners, Christ died for us" (Romans 5:8).

The amazing truth of God's grace is that Jesus chose to suffer for us. He chose the soldier's mocking words and their hateful blows. He chose the way of the cross out of love for us, and we confess that it is because of our sin that He had to endure all this suffering. Confession and sorrow are the only appropriate ways for us to respond to the soldier's treatment of Jesus. They didn't understand, but we do: Jesus suffered and died in our place, taking the penalty of our sin on himself so that we can be set free. Thanks be to God for the life-giving grace we receive through Jesus our Savior!

Father in Heaven, You love me far more than I deserve, and You bless me more than I could ever repay. Thank You for sending Jesus to be my Savior. Help me to honor His name by how I live and to share His story with those in need of salvation. I pray in His wonderful name. Amen.

Matthew 27:45-50

From noon until three in the afternoon darkness came over all the land. About three in the afternoon Jesus cried out in a loud voice, "Eli, Eli, lema sabachthani?" (which means "My God, my God, why have you forsaken me?").

When some of those standing there heard this, they said, "He's calling Elijah."

Immediately one of them ran and got a sponge. He filled it with wine vinegar, put it on a staff, and offered it to Jesus to drink. The rest said, "Now leave him alone. Let's see if Elijah comes to save him."

And when Jesus had cried out again in a loud voice, he gave up his spirit.

I imagine we have all felt forsaken at times, but not like Jesus. It hurts when those you love seem to have forgotten you or when people you thought you could trust seem to abandon you in a moment of need. Those are deeply painful violations of what binds us to other people. To be forsaken is to be left for dead. That's where Jesus was on the cross, but his sorrow went far deeper than any breach of trust we may experience. For Jesus, it was God the Father who looked away as He died. The theological implications of this are profound, as the Trinity seems to have fractured. The Son felt cut off from the Father, a condition never before and never again to be experienced by the Godhead, Three in One. Aside from the shocking theological reality of that moment, Jesus also suffered more grievously than any person ever has. In his humanity, Jesus felt the torment of death physically, emotionally and spiritually.

When Jesus cried out, He was quoting Psalm 22, a prophetic passage that describes a number of the indignities that Jesus endured, including the agony of death on a cross. As hard as it is for us to understand how God could forsake Jesus, it is also remarkable that this was God's own plan, decided upon long beforehand and prophesied about in the Old Testament. God turned away from Jesus on the cross, not because He couldn't bear to watch or because He felt defeated by the forces that nailed his Son there. No, God looked away because Jesus had taken our sin on himself, allowing the curse and filth of our transgressions to cover his holy, righteous body. "God made him who had no sin to be sin for us" (2 Corinthians 5:21), and in that moment, God couldn't look at or be near his beloved Son.

As we contemplate this terrible scene, we need to remember why Jesus went to the cross and what He accomplished there for us. Jesus chose to die in our place, suffering so we would not have to bear the eternal burden of our sin. He was forsaken so we will never be. The sorrow of the cross is also the promise of God's perfect, gracious love. How much does He love you? Enough to send his Son to suffer and die, even to be cut off from the Father's presence. Jesus took all that pain on himself for you, me and everyone who will put their trust in him. Jesus was forsaken and He died, but we know that's not the end of the story...

Father, I struggle to understand how You could love me this much. Thank You for sending Jesus to be my Savior. Thank You for grace, forgiveness and salvation. I rejoice in Your love and commit my heart to follow Jesus today and forever. Amen.

Matthew 28:1-7

After the Sabbath, at dawn on the first day of the week, Mary Magdalene and the other Mary went to look at the tomb.

There was a violent earthquake, for an angel of the Lord came down from heaven and, going to the tomb, rolled back the stone and sat on it. His appearance was like lightning, and his clothes were white as snow. The guards were so afraid of him that they shook and became like dead men.

The angel said to the women, "Do not be afraid, for I know that you are looking for Jesus, who was crucified. He is not here; he has risen, just as he said. Come and see the place where he lay. Then go quickly and tell his disciples: 'He has risen from the dead and is going ahead of you into Galilee. There you will see him.' Now I have told you."

While an earthquake shook the ground and opened the tomb, Jesus' resurrection shook the whole world. That moment changed everything, for everyone, everywhere. No event in history matters as much. No news has ever caused so much joy. Jesus, who was crucified, has risen, just as He said He would. Even 2,000 years later, we still feel the reverberations of that earthquake. Jesus is risen!

Mary and Mary arrived at the tomb at dawn, just as the sun was rising on that Sunday morning. Christian tradition, following the practice of the earliest believers, calls for us to gather for worship on Sundays, the first day of the week. We celebrate Easter once each year, but every Sunday morning worship service is a celebration of the Resurrection. We believe Jesus is with us as the body of believers gathers. His Spirit moves among us, inspiring our praise, comforting us in times of sorrow, and filling us with wisdom from God's word. Jesus welcomes us, hears our prayers, fills us with love, and reminds us of the mission He gave the church to go and make disciples. All this is true because Jesus rose from the dead, just as He said.

If you love and believe in Jesus, this is your story. Jesus' resurrection is the preface and the central theme of your life, and it will provide the heavenly postscript to your earthly life. Your identity, your calling, the very essence of who you are all flow from what happened that Sunday morning at the empty tomb. Jesus is risen! Therefore, you have new life. Therefore, you can know and love God. Therefore, you will overcome the troubles of this world. Therefore, you can live each day with purpose. Therefore, you have hope for eternity. Therefore, you are held safely, now and forever, in the loving, strong arms of God.

Glorious Father, thank You for raising Jesus from the dead and for giving me the hope of eternal life in His name. Your power and grace overwhelm me, and I rejoice today in the good news that my Savior is risen! I love You and commit my heart to follow Jesus forever, as I pray in His mighty name. Amen.

Matthew 28:8-10

So the women hurried away from the tomb, afraid yet filled with joy, and ran to tell his disciples. Suddenly Jesus met them. "Greetings," he said. They came to him, clasped his feet and worshiped him. Then Jesus said to them, "Do not be afraid. Go and tell my brothers to go to Galilee; there they will see me."

How do you think you will respond when you first see Jesus? I imagine your initial face-to-face encounter with the Risen Savior will take place in the glory of heaven. Maybe you will see Jesus at a distance and go running to embrace him. Maybe his appearance will be so majestic that you will not know how to approach him. Whatever He looks like and whatever the heavenly scenery may be, I'm sure we will all treat Jesus the same way the women did after leaving the empty tomb. They fell at his feet, wrapped their arms around him and worshiped. These women had gone to the tomb to perform final burial rites, knowing in the predawn hours that Jesus was dead and his body sealed inside the tomb. They went there that morning with sorrowful hearts, but then, after encountering the angel and seeing the stone rolled away from the empty tomb, they ran off "afraid yet filled with joy." That's when they first saw the Risen Lord and worshiped him.

Everything changed in that moment. The women, along with the other disciples, had known and loved Jesus as their teacher. They had witnessed his miracles and been inspired by his words. They had shared meals with Jesus and discussed the wonders of God. They had decided to follow Jesus, even starting to believe that He was the Messiah prophesied about in scripture. But then He was taken from them and brutally killed. All that they had hoped for seemed crushed and lost forever in the cold stone of that tomb. The shadowy sadness of death hung over them, until "suddenly Jesus met them." In that wonderful moment, as joy eclipsed fear, their faith sprang blonde hair mixing together.

Jess arched, tearing her mouth from Elena's. Eric felt her squeeze down on him, a silent command from her body to his to stay. She cried out. Feeling her coming around him, Eric gasped her name and spent himself.

After her husband and her girlfriend had vigorously reconnected with each other, Elena found herself the center of their attention.

Sweetly kissing her, Eric cradled her back against his chest. He twisted and massaged her nipples, nibbling on her neck while Jess fingered and licked her. Then, after she came twice, inhaling deeply of the sex and sweat in the air, Elena asked, "Both of you, fill me. Please."

Jess stepped away from the bed, getting the strap-on. Eric hummed in Elena's ear as they watched Jess adjust the leather and insert one of the more modest dildos.

Turned over Eric's body by Jess's hands, Elena writhed against his soft chest, the hair stimulating nerve endings and making her even wetter. Working with her fingers, Jess lubed and loosened her ass while Eric's cock returned to attention against her belly. He put on a fresh condom then lifted her up and slid inside her pussy.

Jess cupped Elena's breasts and wrapped herself around Elena until her breasts pressed into Elena's back. Looking down into Eric's blue eyes, feeling his hands on her hips while Jess pulled at her nipples and nibbled at her throat, Elena felt her pussy pulsing in time to her heartbeat around his cock. Pressing her forward and down, Jess's fingers tracing down her spine. When her hands met Eric's on Elena's hips, his hands slid away and she felt him squeezing the cheeks of her ass before kissing her and holding her open for Jess's penetration.

The slow slide of the stiff silicone cock made her belly quiver. Part of her wanted to demand a fast, possessive fuck. More of her, however, felt Jess's kiss to her shoulder blades, heard the sweetly murmured, "I love you," and wanted nothing more than to stay this way for as long as possible.

Curled against Elena's back, Jess minutely moved her hips, taking them both on a slow climb to orgasm. Soft kisses against her nape sparked tingles down Elena's spine. Consciously she squeezed down on Eric's cock. Looking into his blue eyes, she said, "Love you." He arched his neck, his head tilting back, and she kissed his throat. His fingers flexed on her ass and Jess groaned as the motion loosened Elena's passage further and she slid deeper without effort.

Elena reached back, catching Jess's hip and squeezing. "Fuck me," she requested.

A little reorganization, Eric bending his knees to lift his thighs and Jess inching forward on her knees to push in Elena's ass to the base of the strap-on, and Elena felt her orgasm start to ripple from deep in her belly. Both her ass and pussy spasmodically clenched around both her lovers' cocks.

"God, yess," she breathed, her heart starting to pound.

While Eric had gotten hard again, he wasn't coming as quickly, so he remained hard even as Elena and Jess reached orgasm.

Jess pulled out and Elena felt cool air on her open asshole before Jess wrapped her arms around her, hugged her back, and Eric slid out. Elena was now between them. She reached down and massaged Eric's cock in her fist until he came.

Eric reached down and pulled up the sheet over their bodies. Snuggled into his shoulder, she felt Jess press a kiss to her shoulder blade. The bed dipped a moment. Elena heard Jess move away. The strap-on thumped lightly against the porcelain of the bathroom sink. After the bed dipped again, Jess's arm slid again over Elena's hip and her body snuggled up, the hairs of her mound lightly tickling Elena's ass.

Chapter Thirty-One

ELENA STEPPED out of the car and looked up at the office building. Near the top was a cruise line logo. They were willing to talk about reserving a stateroom block for the tour trips. She just had to show them the reservation numbers and make a pitch for reserving one of their smaller on-board restaurants for a kickoff dinner.

"Good afternoon." She smiled at the receptionist. "Elena Tanner. I have a one-thirty with Vincent."

The redhead stood quickly and gestured. "Mr. Danke told us to expect you. Right this way."

Elena followed her down the corridor to a wood grain door with a V. Danke placard in the middle. The redhead knocked.

"Who is it?"

"Ms. Tanner," she replied through the door.

The door opened and a Black man in a gray suit smiled at her. "Ms. Tanner," he said. "Please come in."

"It's Missus," she clarified. "Thank you."

Vincent stayed at the door. "Thanks, Lynn," he said, sending the admin off and closing the door.

Elena sat in the guest chair on the near side of the desk.

Sitting down in his chair, he leaned forward. "I'm glad you

could stop by. Your proposal intrigues me."

"I'm glad. I think there's a real opportunity for everyone in this."

"Whatever your numbers, there will be two more," he said.

"Really?"

"My husband and I are interested."

Elena's eyebrow went up.

"Is that a problem?"

"No, no, of course not. I...I didn't expect."

"That a Black man would be gay, or that an executive in a cruise line would be interested in a swingers gathering?"

"Either. Both, I guess." She lifted her shoulders then dropped them. "Are you serious?"

He chuckled. "Yes. Show me what you've got."

She opened her folio and passed across the desk several sheets of paper. He hummed as he read and the flutter in her chest gradually calmed.

Eric and Jess were working in the backyard when their phones vibrated in their pockets. Jess dropped the mower handle and the engine cut off. Eric lowered the electric saw from the live oak tree branch he had been working on.

Two more guests and we have a cruise block! Elena's text said. *He wants to know if we'll have other gay couples.*

Eric texted, *tell him about you and Jess.*

"I can't go," Jess said.

"We'll see," Eric replied. He kissed her. "Let's get this done and clean up so we can celebrate when Elena gets home."

"You know Cris and Caitlyn have already committed," Eric said.

"I think they wanted to know about male couples, Eric," Jess said.

"There aren't a lot in the lifestyle," Elena said. "I think we've met maybe three, and they were all single, at Caliente."

"What about a bi guy?" Jess asked.

"Even rarer," Eric said.

"I can put out an ad on the bulletin board that LGBTQ are welcome specifically," Elena said.

"Are this guy and his husband going to pull out, if you can't sign some gay tourists?"

Elena looked thoughtful for a moment then shook her head. "I don't think so. He genuinely seemed supportive of the entire project."

"So you have a sponsorship?" She nodded. He leaned over and kissed her cheek. "Congratulations."

Eric stood in front of the large mirror hanging on the wall by the front door and checked the knot on his tie before shrugging into his flight uniform jacket. He sighed as he buttoned it up the front. The doctor had said he'd need to exercise more as his testosterone levels changed. He'd always rationalized away another snack by telling himself all the vigorous sex would counteract any possible pounds, but he had to admit he was thicker around the middle than he liked.

"You look great."

Eric turned away from the mirror to see Jess leaning on the wall sipping from a mug. In it was probably the coffee he'd left in the pot instead of filling his travel mug today. He'd gotten used to getting up at a leisurely time and not needing the caffeine boost to be wide awake.

Jess looked beautiful, sleep tousled, with her hair falling partially across her face. She wore a green tank top and shorts. Lean long legs crossed one bare foot over the other. Green eyes looked at him from over the rim of the mug.

"Didn't mean to wake you," he said.

"You didn't. I wanted, well," she hesitated. "I wanted to say I hope you have a good day at work." She then seemed to laugh at herself. "It's silly."

Eric shook his head. He didn't think it was silly at all. It warmed his heart to know she cared enough to wake up and see him off. He held out a hand and when she put the one without the mug in it, he drew her forward. He cleared his throat. "It's not silly. Thank you."

"Yeah?"

"Yeah." He watched her gaze move over his face and when she looked at his mouth, he lifted her chin and kissed her. "See you tonight."

Jess's skin flushed with heat and her cheeks turned pink. "When you reach New York, text us. I know Elena will want to know you got off okay, too."

"I will." Eric stepped back, looked in the mirror and put on his flight uniform cap. "See you tonight."

"See you."

With light steps, he exited the house. He heard the lock rasp into place as he stepped off the stoop to walk around to the side drive where he kept the car.

Eric had called. The plane used on his flight to the northeast had to be inspected and another was being moved from the secondary hub in Chicago for the return flight pattern. He told them to expect him around midnight.

Jess had gone to her class after an early dinner of cold cuts with Elena. When she got in, she showered then joined Elena in the living room. Together they watched the last half hour of an angsty new adult movie on Netflix.

As the time crept closer to eleven and they exhausted topics about their day and the movie, Elena's yawning finally prompted Jess to kiss her and tell her to go to bed. She wasn't as tired, had some reading to do for class anyway, and would wait up for Eric.

Elena's good night kiss lingered on Jess's lips after Elena had disappeared and she heard the door to the master bedroom shut. Opening her textbook, she pulled her highlighter set from a pocket in her shoulder bag. She had learned to highlight, then organize the ideas with a pen and paper outline. Finally she would transfer the notes onto her laptop for viewing during the online study group.

Eleven became midnight and Eric still hadn't arrived home. Jess went to the front table tray and brought her and Elena's phones back to the living room sofa in case a text from him popped up. She returned to her reading.

Stepping inside the house, Eric forced out the long day with a long exhale. He closed the front door by slowly but firmly pressing it into the jamb. Turning around he placed the convertible's keys in the front table tray. He had already started removing his uniform in the car and now took the jacket and hat from under his arm. Opening the front closet, he took the time to align the jacket on a hanger and hang the hat from a hook. This being his house he decided to take off his pants in the hallway, also settling them onto a hanger in the closet. He loosened and removed his tie, unbuttoned his uniform shirt, putting them both on a third hanger.

He would take the whole ensemble to the dry cleaner tomorrow, and run some polish over his shoes, which was fine since he didn't have another flight assignment for three days.

Hearing the A/C kick in he turned and started across the floor in his underwear and socks. Around the end of the entry wall, he turned toward the bedrooms. He stopped abruptly when out of the corner of his eye, he caught sight of blonde hair visible on the couch. He wondered what Jess had been doing up late. Looking down at her slumped form he deduced from the spread of books and papers across her lap and the surrounding cushions that she had fallen asleep while studying.

A pen rolled out of her limp fingers and hit the floor. Jess jerked awake at the sound. Looking around to see what had happened, her eyes widened when she saw Eric.

"Hi," Eric said softly. "You should probably go to bed."

She rubbed her face and shook her head. "Was waiting up for you."

"You didn't have to."

"I sent Elena to bed at eleven." Jess looked around. When she found and picked up her phone, she exclaimed, "It's nearly two. Wow. What happened?"

"The plane they sent was delayed by a storm front and then we had a few passengers who wanted to argue about boarding delays."

"I'm sorry you had problems."

"It's not your fault. Really, you didn't have to wait up." Eric took Jess's hand as she stepped around the couch. "Did you have class tonight?"

"Yeah." She leaned against the back of the couch.

Eric mirrored her position a few feet away against a side table and crossed his arms over his chest. "I'm trained for all sorts of weather. Don't worry."

"I'm glad." Jess sighed and rubbed her face again.

"You really should go to bed," he repeated.

"You too."

They hugged and he closed his eyes, enjoying the simple contact of affection. Then he took her hand and they walked together into the bedroom hallway. She left him at the master bedroom door and he watched over her short walk to her room.

When Jess was safely inside her bedroom, Eric quietly opened the door to the master bedroom and slipped inside. He glanced toward the bed to confirm he hadn't awakened Elena and moved quickly past the bed into the bathroom. A shower might wake her, but that couldn't be helped. He was determined to be quick about it. While Jess's hug had hastened his unwinding, he was muscle-sore and needed the steam to clear his head.

Chapter Thirty-Two

SEEING JESS making headway with her life, Elena focused her efforts with her business. After securing the cruise block, she was close to locking in all the sponsors and clients she needed. Then in an almost magical moment, calculator in hand, she realized the sponsorship she had just secured from BD Services had put her over the top. It was time for an official launch. She really wanted everyone to mix and mingle at a club party, feeling the energy created would have people eager to sign on for future trips.

She went to call Caliente to reserve a night for a party and then remembered Hector and Maya would probably not be welcoming. In her emails with Caitlyn, she'd learned someone reported prostitution and they'd closed their doors. In truth though that couldn't make her depressed. For the first time she felt her life was truly balanced. She, Eric, and Jess were settling in together.

After Eric's vasectomy the spontaneity in their sex had resumed in between what had become evenly split chores and work schedules. Jess had gotten a second shift call center job, and got home by eleven. She often pulled Elena to bed where they made love before falling asleep. When Eric came home from his flights on Thursdays, Jess was on her way out for her shift. Elena snuggled with him while he napped. They'd make love when he awoke and make dinner together.

The three of them usually kept Saturdays for yard work as the spring arrived early with summer-like heat. Sundays they gathered in the living room, watching Netflix and chatting, or making out and having sex on the deck, in the playroom, or in the bedroom.

Elena tried to book a couple other clubs for her startup party but from the beginning she had misgivings because she didn't really know them as well. The reticence apparently went both ways because she had no luck lining up there either.

The lack of a public venue for her launch meant she was back to considering private ones. She had no budget for a VIP lounge and closed floor reservation at the Hyatt, which would have suited the corporate sponsors.

That left her hosting here at the house. Truthfully, she had thought the house party back in November nearly perfect. She had felt literally "at home" in a way that the club couldn't ever replicate. Time to bring it up to her partners.

She gathered her notes and went out to the backyard. Shirtless and wearing a headband to keep sweat from his eyes, Eric mowed the lawn. Jess had the pool's manual cleaning equipment in her hands and walked around the rim in her new bathing suit. The sight was enough to make Elena's mouth water.

Business first, she reminded herself. "Jess!" she called out, which got Jess's attention easily.

Pausing in her walk, she lifted out the pole and set it down. "Hi. What's up?"

Elena kissed her when Jess reached her side. "I've made my numbers for the first trip. I'd like to host a launch."

Jess's smile was excited and she rubbed the back of Elena's neck with her fingers in praise. "That's great. I'll be happy to help."

"I want to host the meeting here." She paused; Eric had noticed the two of them standing together and cut the mower's engine before striding toward them. She looked over to him. "As a house party."

"What house party?" he asked.

"I want to bring everyone together. Have the first tour group's official launch here."

"I thought you were going to arrange to go to a club?"

"Couldn't find one. Caliente, as you know, is closed. The others just...don't have the right feel."

Eric sat down on a lounger by the pool. The move drew Jess to sit also. Elena remained standing, looking from one to the other.

"Hosting here means we can transition from meeting to mingling more naturally. I'll rent chairs. We can have everyone in the backyard, barbecue and all. Then when the socializing starts..."

"We won't know everyone though. You have only talked with some on the phone, right? The rest were internet sign ups."

"True. But—"

"We set firm ground rules," Eric said.

"Of course. We had them last time."

"We'll go over them again. Make sure there isn't something we overlooked." He kissed her then Jess as his arms came around them both.

"Get a load of you!" Jess stepped out of her room to find Eric lifting his hands and preening for her in a spicy red polyester suit with tuxedo shirt, ruffles gaily bouncing.

She grabbed the wide lapels of his suit and pressed herself full length against him, assaulting him with her lips. "So hot, Eric," she purred in his ear.

He separated and took in her chosen costume for the evening. "Love the mondo shades," he complimented, "but it's a shame they hide your gorgeous green eyes." His gaze scanned down her pale blue suit and paused, she knew, on the bulge in her pants. "Does Elena know you decided to pack tonight?"

"Fits my role," Jess said with a smile. "I'm going to be here at the door. Checking ID and invitations." She flexed, which looked a little strange as 'Elton John' but Eric got the picture. Jess had taken the initiative yet again, taking on the role of 'bouncer' and enforcer of the party rules.

He reached out and squeezed her arm muscle. She squeaked and he kissed her.

The door to the master bedroom opened. Jess and Eric turned to the knee-buckling sight of Elena stepping out in a sleek form-fitted sailor-styled blue and white skirt and top. The 1970s styled scupper hat was pinned jauntily to her sleekly styled ebony hair specially waved and held with hairspray for the occasion. Jess's whistle melded with Eric's in nearly perfect low-pitch harmony.

"Fancy a night on the town, sailor?" Eric asked.

"I'm interested in a night inside, Mr. Candy Man. You got something sweet for me?"

"Always rocking the sweet stuff, my salty wench," he bantered back.

Elena stepped up to Jess and clung to her right arm, sliding a hand down her pale blue wide lapel suit. She pressed into Jess from hips to breasts and smirked. Eric knew Elena had not missed the presence of Jess's strap-on. Her words confirmed it. "So, Bennie wants to get the jets going tonight?"

"Engine's revved and ready," Jess assured. "You're covering the rules in the introduction session, after talking about the cruise, right?"

"Yes. I've got my presentation and notes all here." Elena went to a box on the dining table. "My business cards, program pamphlets, and the registration packets all came in." She showed off the professionally printed materials. "Got my safety speech as well as all the ice breakers and party games prepared, too."

"You do look the part of the sexy cruise director," he praised and kissed her cheek. "I'm going to set up for my role as chef."

"Jess?"

"I'm right here by the door."

Elena pulled off Jess's glasses and kissed her nose right between her green eyes. "Thank you."

"You're welcome." Jess took back her glasses and stepped back. Elena pulled a tri-fold of wood panels across the hallway leading to their rooms. While everyone would be allowed in the living room, kitchen, out on the pool and deck, and eventually the playroom downstairs, their bedrooms would be off-limits.

Checking IDs against the list and putting wristbands on each guest kept Jess near the door for the first twenty-five minutes. Eric and Elena passed around hors d'oeuvres and drinks, which were non-alcoholic until the presentation was finished.

Jess checked the clock after a run of five guests who had all piled out of two more cars and locked the door. No one would be allowed to enter once things started. They weren't going to repeat the party rules or the presentation. Elena had collected security deposits from these people already as a way to gauge their commitment. She counted on her checklist as she walked toward the back of the house where Elena was already making her way toward the table set up for her to speak.

"Good evening, everyone. Some of you already know me well. For the rest, I'm Elena Tanner and I want to thank you for coming out tonight to the launch of an exciting new venture in adult travel packaging: Tanner Travel."

Jess stood behind the back row, nodding to a few guests, but mostly she looked around as people applauded, listening to Elena repeat her introduction in Spanish. A few nodded more vigorously at the revelation of Elena's bilingual skills. They followed as she talked about her desire to fill a niche market and detailed the first all-inclusive package trip to a U.S. Virgin Islands resort flying out of Miami. She translated herself in Spanish before every change in topic.

Jess stood a couple times when she saw people getting up and moving toward the house. In most cases, they were refilling drinks or getting more hors d'oeuvres. Eric was actually at the back door since he was monitoring the grill and already pulling off hamburgers and hot dogs and setting them in warming trays.

Elena looked flushed but pleased when she finished and received applause. She announced food and the downstairs playroom was available. She reminded them that they had signed 'house rules' agreements to be here, and asked if there were any questions. She waited for someone to crack a crass joke, or ask if such-n-such obviously outside the rules thing would be allowed. No one did. Elena had clearly done a good job screening people who were serious about the lifestyle and flush enough to travel.

She noticed a few familiar faces including the married women Cris and Caitlyn, which she remembered meeting at the Tanners' first house party back in November as well as at the Caliente's costume party a few months ago. They nodded at her and she lifted her glass in return before continuing to walk through the backyard.

"Is the pool open?"

She turned toward the speaker, finding a slender redheaded man in a well-fitted dark blue suit. He wore a pale blue button up, open at the neck. "No, I'm sorry, the pool isn't open for today. We thought it would be too chilly once the sun set. And too much hassle for changing space."

"You're probably right. So you work with Ms. Tanner?" He held out his hand. "I'm Barry Dawson. My company is one of the sponsors."

"Which company?" Jess asked.

"BD Services. We do set design."

"I'm glad you cleared that up," Jess said.

"Why? What did you think we did?"

"BDSM."

"I get that a lot, actually. I have built a number of dungeons in the area."

"Are you comfortable with that?"

"A set is a set," he replied with a shrug. "I was a theater major in college and worked a lot of the Miami playhouses until I could start my own business."

"Elena did her own layout and decorating for their basement."

"Have you been there?"

"Not yet tonight."

"But you have been there?" Barry asked. "Would you like to show me around?"

"I'm hosting," Jess replied, offering a gracious, honest, cue to withdraw. "Have a good evening."

He smiled and gave her a nod. "Thank you."

A few minutes later, Jess was seated in the living room's corner couch, sipping a second small glass of wine and chatting with a gay male couple. Marcus was an executive in an adult film company that had agreed to be a movie night sponsor for this first trip.

Between one sip and the next, Elena settled onto her lap and kissed her. Jess tucked her free arm around Elena's waist, sliding her fingers beneath the sailor suit and stroking the heated bare skin at Elena's waist.

"Come dance with me, Bennie," Elena said in a gorgeously affected Brooklyn accent.

Chuckling, Jess downed the last of her wine, clearing her palette. She turned to accept Elena's mouth on hers again, sucking on the tongue that quickly emerged. Elena was already quivering with need, so Jess made their excuses. "Enjoy yourselves," she said to the two men. "Marcus and..." She trailed off.

"Greg," the darker of the couple said. "You too. We'll see you again."

Elena lifted herself from Jess's lap and then grabbed her hands, pulling Jess to her feet. "C'mon." They moved to the open space by the sound system where other couples were dancing to the Bee Gees. Elena had been determined to create a full-on 1970s theme. Jess pulled Elena into her arms, hands lifting the tiny white sailor skirt, and massaging the woman's ass as they danced and kissed.

"I'm glad you found them. They're really excited for your business," Jess said.

"I was just downstairs showing Barry around," Elena said.

"Barry? The set designer I met earlier?"

"Yes. He's going to help me with some of the theme nights."

Elena's hands were sneaking inside her suit. With a smile, Jess asked, "Are you horny from the energy of the creative conversation or seeing everyone who's already gone down to have sex?"

"Elton, I need your fingers to play me *right now*," Elena bantered back.

Dipping her head, Jess nosed up under Elena's jaw, nibbling and kissing at the throbbing pulse in the woman's throat. She turned and pulled Elena close so she was reminded of the presence of Jess's strap-on. "Just my fingers?"

"Which one are you wearing?" Elena asked.

"Feeldoe."

"And you've been walking around..." Elena whimpered.

When she pulled back to gauge the effect of her words, Elena's brown gaze was as heated as Jess had ever seen. All right then. She smiled and squeezed the ass cupped in her palms. "Playroom?"

"Playroom," Elena confirmed.

Downstairs the playroom was busy and noisy with sounds of sex and laughter. The air was laden with cinnamon scent from the candles burning to keep the atmosphere intimate. Jess took off her glasses and tucked them in the suit's oversized pocket. Bodies writhed and panted on the numerous mattresses and cushions. The "harem" space had a maharajah hat peeking out between the sheer drapes coming down from the ceiling. At the swing, a blond man and woman were taking turns fingering and fucking a voluptuous redhead woman who pulled at the ropes and made herself swing more vigorously onto the woman's hand, even as she grunted demanding, "More!"

Jess smiled and recalled her own times in that swing and the freedom to just take and take, never worrying about feeling too needy.

Elena led Jess to a set of play pillows, wedges and sheets. Eric's dark blond figure was easily recognizable on another set of pillows nearby. He had a blonde woman with short cropped hair on her hands and knees banging back onto his stiff cock; Jess saw the condom on it glistening each time he slid out. The woman's face contorted with ecstasy when Eric reached around her hip and obviously added to her pleasure with his fingers on her clit.

The woman gasped and dropped her head onto the pillows, leaving her rear in the air. Elena chuckled.

Jess smiled at her and they knelt together on the cushions. "He's so good," Elena said. "But I wanna show off how well you love me," she added, pulling Jess by the lapels until their mouths crashed together. She pulled off the big jacket, but left Jess's thick shirt. She opened the zipper of the pants, releasing the dong. She bent and pulled it into her mouth, cooing as she mouthed it, wetting it thoroughly. The other end of the dong moved inside Jess, stirring up her arousal faster.

Stroking Elena's shoulders, Jess gradually worked the other woman out of the sailor top until she cupped bare breasts in her hands. There was a clasp at the side of the skirt, but for now, Jess pulled it up inches at a time, showing off the fine ass she was about to have to a pair of men nearby who were slyly eyes up even as they ate out their respective partners. Jess admired the pale bodied women, their curves undulating, and glistening with a thin layer of perspiration, and could definitely say she loved most women's looks, as she did many men.

But looking back down to Elena's midnight black hair, intent face, dark lashes fluttering against olive complexion, and the golden skin on her shoulders and back as she flexed, Jess knew that she held a special love for *this* woman.

It was more than her looks. It was the exuberance she brought to life, the playfulness that alternated with a bounty of hard-earned life wisdom. Jess grasped Elena under her shoulders, hauled her up along her body, and latched on with a deep kiss the moment her mouth was within reach.

Clutching Elena's body to her, she bent forward until the woman rested amid the cushions. She reverently stroked breasts and belly all the while continuing to kiss, taking in Elena's welcoming moans and giving back her own while she positioned both of their bodies in the cushions. Lifting Elena's legs over her hips and atop a wedge pillow, she gazed upon a neatly trimmed pussy spread puffy and wet before her. When Jess looked up, smoky brown eyes winked at her.

She stroked, massaged, and squeezed the sleek legs she wanted wrapped around her. Then she guided Elena's ankles behind her back and murmured, "Hold on." Elena crossed her ankles, put her arms around Jess's shoulders, pulled her down, and aligned their bodies. Jess canted her hips and found the tip of her strap-on with her hand between their bellies. With her fingers she found Elena's wetness and lined up the angle with a bit more shifting. All the while she held the other woman's gaze, mesmerized by the swirls of flickering candlelight cast from the nearby motley collection on a small tabletop. She lifted a condom from a box beside them on the floor. Elena took it, tore it open, and unrolled it over the Feeldoe.

Jess jerked slightly and gasped; Elena smirked at the result of finding Jess's clit. In reply, Jess lifted the Feeldoe's tip and slid it up and down the lips of Elena's center. Everything became slick with the woman's essence.

When Elena tapped her shoulder, Jess took the cue and slid smoothly inside on one deep stroke. She rocked her hips, moving minutely while she circled Elena's clit with her thumb. Elena hooked her ankles behind Jess's back. She lifted her hips and fucked herself, creating the sensual sight for Jess of Elena's pussy swallowing the dong's length. The sight was such a turn-on that Jess growled and grabbed Elena's breast, twisting the nipple between her fingers. Elena gave an incoherent cry and her head and shoulders rolled back, pushing her breasts upward.

Leaning forward, Jess pulled on the gorgeously thick nipples, alternately twisting and pinching, while continuing to rock forward and back, stroking both of them deeply with each movement. Finally she released Elena's breasts and unlocked Elena's arms from around her neck.

"Is this all right?" she asked as she adjusted Elena's body to take her deeper still.

Elena's nod was quick. Her throaty, "Fill me," gave Jess permission to thrust long and deep, pushing the dong until she felt the woman's pubic hairs against her own inner thighs. She was all the way in. Teasing Elena, she pulled out slowly before pushing back quickly. Elena grunted and pulled on her hair. Continuing to listen and feel Elena's responses, Jess repeated the motions: slow out, fast in.

At the deepest point of her most recent push, Jess could hear Elena's panting signaled she was close to orgasm. Slight resistance inside herself told her Elena's inner muscles were eagerly grasping the other end. The fast out made Elena gasp when her muscles tried to grab again but were denied. Brown eyes flashed and her mouth opened in an 'O', which Jess immediately claimed in a kiss.

"Wanna make this last," she said when she parted from nibbling Elena's bottom lip. "Boost yourself up a bit."

Elena raised onto her elbows, lifting her upper body. With her hands more free, Jess switched to slow fucking. In at a snail's pace, she rotated her hips while equally slowly backing out. She teased Elena's clit with her fingertips and watched the woman's pussy stretching around the dong's girth. Jess's gut clenched and she felt an orgasm spike pleasure from her groin into her legs, making them shake.

Cupping Jess's cheeks, Elena spoke into her mouth, "Jess?"

"Yes?" Jess said, panting as she maintained the slow rhythm of the fuck.

"I want you..." Elena's voice trailed off as Jess knew it would from the dual sensations she was delivering to the woman's clit and throat with her fingers and tongue.

"Yeah, I know you want me," Jess teased, nipping at Elena's throat. "but how would you like to have me?"

"Oh, god, don't stop," Elena gasped as the next stroke hit a particular spot. Jess grinned proudly. Elena laughed and teased, "Cocky is such a good look for you."

Jess rotated her hips while pulling out and pushing back in. Elena's fingers squeezed at her shoulders. "So?" she reminded. "What do you want?"

"Just fuck me until I can't think straight anymore."

"You never thought straight to begin with," Jess teased back, but she began working the dong in earnest, pulling out until the bulbous head rubbed against Elena's lips and then pushing back in agonizing inches at a time, until she could quickly push the last of the distance, their sweaty skin audibly slapping together.

She looked around to see if their actions were being noticed. Elena had wanted to show her off after all. A few of the men's eyes roved over her and Elena, but it was Eric's blue eyes reaching out the few feet between them that Jess most appreciated. He nodded, twitching his mustache with a wide smile, just as Jess felt a tug on her shirt.

"Need you." Elena sloppily pulled open Jess's shirt, losing a few buttons but releasing the binding on her breasts. Jess cried out in pleasure as her breasts were first massaged, then pulled and twisted, and finally sucked. She repeatedly slammed her hips forward as a way to release the rising need as Elena sucked on her nipples.

Shutting her eyes, she dropped her forehead down onto Elena's hair, almost mindless now with the scent of their sex-sweaty bodies surrounding her and the pulling she could feel inside herself as Elena's muscles grabbed at the Feeldoe. She tried to balance on her knees only to feel hands loosening her pants and sliding them off her hips. When the material was bunched around her knees, she knew her ass was on display, the leather straps of the harness bisecting her ass cheeks.

Elena's hands cupped her face again and then slid down her back and took firm hold of the fleshier part of Jess's rear. A bigger hand joined hers on Jess's skin. Looking over her shoulder, Jess saw Eric and his recent female partner sitting behind her, hands on their thighs. One of Eric's hands had joined Elena's on Jess's ass.

"May we join in?" Eric asked.

"Green," Jess said positively. Eric leaned forward and his kiss was deep and sweet, and she sighed when she felt his hand caress her hair. That hand finally ventured lower, coming between Jess's ass cheeks, spreading the wetness he found as he encountered the Feeldoe. She glanced toward the blonde Eric had been with earlier and nodded in greeting.

The woman returned the regard with smiling blue eyes. "Caitlyn."

"Jess," she replied, now recalling the woman she had met several times before. They hadn't been this close up before. "You have a partner named Cris, right?"

"Yes. She's over there." Caitlyn replied, her thumb tossing toward a couple, the male fucking a woman doggy style over a cushion.

A pull on the half-Windsor knot that had taken her nearly twenty minutes to perfect brought Jess's attention back to Elena. She moved her hips and grinned when Elena did the same. "I want to see you both fuck her," Elena said.

Caitlyn looked from Jess to Eric. "He told me. I'm in."

"Jess?" Eric asked.

"I'm game. You're going to be doing all the hard work though." She chuckled and withdrew herself from Elena slowly. Laying on her back, she coaxed Elena to straddle her shoulders with a pat. "I get a delicious mouthful of pussy."

Elena settled over her, knees on either side of Jess's head, facing Eric and Caitlyn. Eric helped Caitlyn straddle Jess's hips, removing the used condom from the Feeldoe and letting Caitlyn apply a new one.

Reaching up to guide Elena's hips, Jess pulled her down over her face. She admired the swollen lips for only a moment before she could resist no longer. She swiped her tongue from front to back in random swirls. Elena's hands clutched at her chest, ribs, and waist. Sounds of pleasure continually fell from her lips. Underneath, Jess felt rather than saw Caitlyn lower herself onto the Feeldoe's free end. In a brief space when Caitlyn and Elena pulled back in the midst of adjusting, Jess saw Elena guiding Caitlyn forward, and Eric moving in behind Caitlyn. He fussed at his crotch out of Jess's line of sight likely working on another condom. Jess wondered if Eric was going to take Caitlyn in the ass only until she felt the thickness of his cock pushing across her thigh. She tightened her Kegel muscles to hold the Feeldoe firmly in place while he worked his cock inside Caitlyn alongside the dong. His fingers snuck a caress of Jess's clit just as Elena had done earlier. Caitlyn gasped, but the sound was cut off.

Jess realized Elena probably kissed Caitlyn in the middle of the maneuver because Elena ground down on her face and she knew how turned on Elena got watching Eric fuck. Returning to her pleasurable task of sucking Elena's folds, Jess felt Eric maneuver his dick and her dong, until they were both full length inside Caitlyn. Eric's knees were outside Jess's. The extra pressure helped her keep the Feeldoe in. The woman had obviously been well-prepared already and Jess briefly wondered if she'd taken a DP like this before.

An orgasm started to sneak up on Jess as the Feeldoe was pushed around by Eric's cock. Caitlyn's hips shifted across Jess's, opening herself wider to their dual penetration.

Hands planted on Jess's abs, Caitlyn began raising and dropping herself onto both of them. Eric's hands on Jess's thighs kept him steady. Jess heard the kissing going on above her, followed by a light laugh from Elena and then Eric's fuller chuckle. He started to groan in rhythm and Jess felt a hand brush against her waist. The longer nails told her it was Caitlyn.

Elena tightened above Jess, a sign she was coming. Redoubling her attentions, Jess grasped at Elena's gyrating hips with her hands, and alternated plying the underside of Elena's clit with the tip of her tongue then enthusiastically sucking at it.

Giving a pleased cry, Elena's tightness gave way to weakened limbs. She collapsed forward, her head briefly on Caitlyn's chest until the woman moved away.

Eric lifted Caitlyn up off Jess. He changed his condom and reentered her missionary style next to her and Elena. In moments, Jess heard Caitlyn and Eric coming together, their groans intermingling.

Inhaling the cinnamon and paraffin smells from the candles and the scent of Elena's sex that clung to her face, Jess stroked

Elena's back, reveling in the completely boneless and trusting way the other woman lay against her. Head resting on Jess's hip, Elena's breath ghosted over her damp thighs. Listening to the music and the sounds of sex continuing around them, Jess contentedly closed her eyes.

Elena's fingertips lightly danced on Jess's skin.

"She's adorable," Caitlyn said.

Jess thought about saying something, but gave up thinking. Instead she sank into the contentment of Elena's hand stroking her belly.

Elena's voice slid over her ears and brought tears to her eyes. "Jess is beautiful, inside and out."

Epilogue

"OH, THIS'LL bring out your eyes," Elena said, pulling a light green bikini bathing suit from the rack at the department store. Jess couldn't immediately see how it would be held up over her modest assets, until Elena fingered the thin spaghetti straps that would tie around her neck. Their basket held an already dizzying array of spring wear, shorts, blouses and summer dresses. They were only going away for four days, but Elena seemed determined to buy Jess an entirely new wardrobe.

"Go put it on."

"I've never worn anything like this," Jess said.

"She can go in and help you fit yourself, dear," the matronly sales associate said, not even really looking at them.

Jess caught Elena's eyes twinkling with mischief. Jess took the key from the sales associate and walked down the narrow corridor where doors hid away tiny little dressing rooms. "I can try it on myself," Jess said over her shoulder. "These look kinda cramped for two."

Elena shook her head and guided Jess's hand to the last door on the left. "It'll be perfectly fine."

The door latched behind Elena and Jess caught the small sound of the latch being locked. Jess set down her coat and started to unbutton her shirt. Elena helped her push it from her shoulders, briefly trapping Jess's arms behind her back and stealing a kiss since they were nose to nose. Jess felt the kiss deep in her belly and moaned.

Elena smiled as she trapped the sound against Jess's lips. Then she pulled back and teased Jess's nipples with her fingertips. "Sh, you've got to be quiet. We don't want Miz Matronly to come investigating any sounds."

Feeling Elena squeeze her breasts meaningfully, Jess moaned, laughed, and sighed, happily at the mercy of Elena's wicked sense of humor. Jess bit her lip to keep in the next moan that tried to escape as Elena brushed their bodies together as she reached behind Jess and removed her bra. Jess stuffed her hands in her mouth to stifle sounds when Elena nipped and then sucked at each breast's tip hardening in the air-conditioned air of the store. The sensations were going directly to Jess's center, and by the smirk on her lips, Elena knew it. Jess's hips jerked toward her lover uncontrollably.

Sitting on the tiny corner bench, Elena guided Jess forward by the hips, until she stood between Elena's knees. Elena unsnapped Jess's jeans, pulling down underwear along with the denim.

"I think I'm supposed to keep those —"

Jess's whisper was silenced by her biting her own lip to restrain a moan when Elena's fingers then her tongue toyed with Jess's clit. Jess slapped the wall before remembering where they were and instead slapped both her hands over her mouth. "Mmmffff!" she groaned.

Making pleased sounds, Elena smiled into Jess's flesh and changed the licks to languid strokes, keeping Jess on edge and building her pleasure more slowly.

Pulling thick dark hair between her fingers, Jess fought to stay grounded, even though her knees were shaking. "Elena," she whispered, barely managing both syllables before she was breathless.

"Sit down, Jess."

Elena helped Jess to switch places so Elena now stood above Jess who sank to the bench. An unmistakably hungry look in her brown eyes, Elena lowered to her knees and spread Jess's thighs with long massaging strokes. Then her mouth returned to Jess's sex. Two fingers joined Elena's tongue just as Jess felt the need to clench something.

Resting her head against the dressing room wall, Jess brushed her fingers through Elena's hair, over her cheeks, and along her shoulders, wanting to communicate her pleasure without sounds. Though unintelligible sounds of desire and want still fell from her lips with soft frequency, she wanted to convey her jumbled feelings to the other woman.

Elena captured one hand and, with just one squeeze, Jess felt calm finally settle within her mind.

Squeezing her eyes shut, tears leaked from beneath Jess's lashes. When she opened her eyes again, Elena lifted her chin. Fingers continued moving below and Jess held Elena's gaze. That warm cocoa color became her whole world just as she came.

Jess's orgasm was visceral, a gushing physical release. It was also soft and made her feel like she was floating, like the waters of a brook were tripping over her body. She almost thought she heard the sound of the water in her ears.

Capturing one of Jess's hands, Elena gently tugged and laced their fingers together. Jess squeezed her eyes shut, tears leaking hotly over her cheeks. Fingers resumed moving within her and Jess focused on Elena's eyes as she came again.

Elena sat back on her heels. She smiled and licked Jess's fluids from her fingers. Jess coaxed her up, gesturing her onto her lap. Seeking her mouth now close by, Jess massaged Elena's knees apart, sliding a hand up between parting thighs.

Her fingers were squeezed as she rocked and twisted them inside. Elena came silently. The only sign of exertion was the rapidly ticking pulse in Elena's throat. Jess kissed it. Elena stifled a moan behind her hand and Jess smiled against the skin.

After a few moments snuggling, Jess licked clean her own fingers. She straightened and pulled her fingers through her disarrayed hair. Elena retrieved her shirt. Standing together they replaced their clothing. Jess reached over and picked up the bikini. "I don't really need one for the house pool," she said. "I could just wear the one you loaned me."

"Around the house you could wear nothing at all," Elena murmured against Jess's mouth. "But there's something to be said for stripping you out of it when you're soaking wet."

Jess redressed and they left the dressing room. She put the bikini in the basket with her other purchases. Together they walked to the front of the store and checked out. A point of pride, Jess split the items with Elena and they went through a cashier aisle.

A little while later, Elena pulled the convertible into the driveway and turned to Jess. She took Jess's hand. "We're home," she said.

Home. Jess felt a shiver go down her spine. Elena's face was split in a wide, warm smile that made Jess want to crawl into her arms. She swallowed with awareness.

Feeling dizzy, Jess squeezed Elena's hand. Something crumbled a little in her chest. A hardness that had built up as a result of her life, people coming and going, people who insisted that some new place was her home only for the expected calm to never materialize. That hardness began breaking apart.

Jess looked out to the Spanish-styled house with its gardens and brick walk. Seeing Eric using an electric trimmer on the front hedges she smiled and murmured, "Home."

Elena turned her head and caught her gazing. She reached out and took Jess's hand. "Home."

About the Author

Lara Zielinsky is a bisexual married woman and works from home as a writer and fiction editor. She grew up reading, as it was the one thing as an introvert she could do alone in a house full of people. When she realized these stories weren't reflecting the things she thought about, she started writing her own. She discovered romance books in her teens, particularly looking for stories with strong female leads. When she opened up about her orientation, her stories started reflecting bisexuality. She got her start writing fanfic in the Xenaverse and then drifted into other fandoms. Eventually she started writing original fiction. Her first novel "Turning Point" was published in 2007. "We Fit" (2022) is Lara's fourth published novel through Supposed Crimes (Acquitted Books).

Website: http://larazbooks.com